3/25/19 Thank you for meeting us a

— Live your Life

my new Friend.

e flight to L.A

Derrick J Reed

Mind Set
Go

YOU'RE BIGGER THAN YOU KNOW

Derrick D. Reed

p 25, 30

ISBN: 0692985379

ISBN 13: 9780692985373

Dedication

I dedicate this book first, to my family. God has given me the privilege and the wisdom to be the kind of leader they can love and respect. Words can't express the love I have for you all. I am truly a proud husband and dad. I also dedicate this book to the countless people that support me. My circle and my corner, you know who you are. I just want to make you all proud.

Table of Contents

Introduction

In the summer of 1985, I saw my first movie: *Back to the Future*. While the plot still sticks in my head, the movie itself wasn't the memorable moment for me. My older brother Sam took me and my twin brother, Frederick. As we waited in line, I looked up at the prices of the movies and the snacks; shocked, my first thought was: movie theaters were not a place for kids - *and certainly not poor kids*.

It was that very moment in my life where I knew I wanted to be more. Not only did I not want something as simple as, the price of movies, to shock me - I wanted more from life. However, it wasn't only my life that I wanted to change. If I was going to enjoy life, I wanted others to have the same experience. I didn't want me, or anyone else, to float through life waiting for something good to happen - I wanted to make it happen. While it may seem small, that moment at the movies gave me the drive I needed to push forward in life. It gave me the high drive I needed to create a life far different from the one I was living: a life worth passing on to my children. My new worldview was birthed out of a strong desire to experience FREEDOM and FULFILLMENT, on all levels. My new worldview was the start of MIND SET GO. From understanding the importance of time currency to making sure I have the right people in my corner, MIND SET GO pushed me forward in the world. MIND SET GO is what makes me a success, and now, it will make you one too.

Chapter One

Red or Blue Pill

In the classic scene of the 1999 mega-hit film *The Matrix*, Laurence Fishburne plays the enlightened Morpheus, who gives Neo, played by Keanu Reeves, a choice: the Red Pill or the Blue Pill. The pills represented the decision between remaining where he was in life, based on what he's always been taught and believed, or excelling to the next level of enlightenment, where knowledge and success could be found by knowing and accepting what is *real* truth, based on facts and results.

In today's world, accepting the Blue Pill is the choice of staying average: living with unanswered questions that return, time after time, leaving you unfulfilled. The Red Pill represents TRUTH: the decision to forget what you've been incorrectly taught by the inexperienced, the uneducated, and even the seemingly, educated, from childhood to adulthood.

The Red Pill is a conscious decision to *no longer* accept something as being truth, without evidence. It is knowing that all truth is based on facts, proof, and more importantly, results.

Now, when I say: "forget what you've been taught," I don't mean everything. Whether, you came from a good or bad upbringing, there are still some valuable lessons and experiences that helped you along your journey. However, there will be a time in your life when you will have to ask yourself:

"Who am I?"

"Why am I here?"

"What do I know for myself?"

"What is my purpose?"

At this very point, the "Mind Set Go" mindset begins to take over, reset, restore, gain knowledge, and ultimately CHANGE...YOU. Congratulations you have just chosen the Red Pill.

Most people say when things get right I'll make a move

The Reality is...THINGS GET RIGHT WHEN YOU MAKE A MOVE!

Born in the small city of Wilmington, Delaware, my twin brother and I were the youngest of nine siblings. My parents were married, good old-fashioned, Sunday morning church-folk. My late Father was a self-employed construction worker from Middletown, in the southern part of Delaware.

From as far as I can remember, my mother, who was born in Detroit, Michigan, and raised in Greenville, South Carolina, was a stay-at-home mom. Sadly, they divorced around the time my brother and I turned five. Because my father was the breadwinner, it didn't take long for things to take a downward spiral. After he left, we ended up living in various places: motels, emergency housing, and even with strangers who opened their homes, and allowed us to stay from time to time. Eventually, we landed in the Riverside Housing Projects on the east side of Wilmington, Delaware.

Until that point, we didn't know much about being poor, or even struggling. My mom did the best she knew how on raising us, and by that time, just about all of our older siblings had grown up and moved on with their lives. Moving from place to place became the norm. Dealing with the constant change of lifestyle was a little depressing at times, and without my father there, my mother developed a drinking habit. Unfortunately, on top of home life, the neighborhood was broken, drug-infested, and crime-filled; we had to learn how to be street smart, *real quick*.

Poverty comes with many challenges. Getting dressed was one of these challenges. I remember getting ready for school, growing up, and trying to find something to wear. I had to wear the same clothes two, sometimes, three times a week. As soon as we walked in the door from school, we would hear our mother say, "Get out them school clothes," and we did. We tried not to wear the same clothes again until later in the week, but sometimes, jeans were worn again the very next day.

Being embarrassed about my appearance, even as a young kid, wasn't just about the clothes we wore or borrowed, but how I looked in general. I felt like I was imprisoned by my appearance. Inside, I knew I was outgoing, I knew I had a great personality, an outstanding sense of humor and was very intelligent. However, no one would have known because I was so embarrassed by my skinny body, tremendous overbite, and my large sized teeth. Held hostage by my appearance, I wouldn't let go and allow myself to be in the spotlight in any shape, form, or fashion. Plus, I'm sure you can imagine how cruel kids were at such young ages.

Then, there was my hair; my hair really embarrassed me. I probably got my hair cut once a month, only after it grew out to a nappy-ass, impossible-to-comb, afro. I can remember going to the barbershop maybe once. For the most part, we got our hair cut by a local barber that cut inside of his bedroom, not too far from our house. He wasn't a licensed barber or anything, he was more like that uncle with a bunch of side hustles; cutting the neighborhood kids was just one of them. I'll mention more about him in just a second.

One day, I woke up to get ready for school, and realized it was picture day (I HATED PICTURE DAY). My hair wasn't cut, and I couldn't find anything to wear (trust me this story gets worse). I recall staring at the top drawer and nothing was in there! The second drawer? Nothing! Third drawer? Socks and underwear.

Then I came to the fourth drawer. I pulled it open and there was my all time I-HATE-THESE-PANTS-FOREVER, pants in the bottom drawer. I almost cried because the moment I saw them, I knew I was going to have to put them on (of course, my mom loved those pants). They were red and white, small checkered printed pants, and they fit really tightly.

My mom would say, "Boy, there ain't nothing wrong with them pants, just throw on a white shirt." (Is it just me, or did parents back then NOT have an inkling idea as to what kids went through in elementary school, especially when their appearance was out of whack from top to bottom - *or did they just NOT care?* I mean, did they not know that kids would clown you for wearing HIGH WATER pants, stains on shirts, hair not done, or played-out sneakers. Yes, these things DO MATTER in a kid's life!! Okay, I just felt the need to let that out, let's continue...)

So, I found a white shirt and went into the bathroom to look in the mirror. While putting on the shirt, which actually didn't look bad, I realized that my hair wasn't cut. As a matter of fact, it had been at least, a little over a month since I had my last haircut done by, "Q," the bootleg bar-ber I told you about. In case you don't know, "bootleg" is what we call anyone who operates in a profession without a license – *funny.*

Although he was really good, and probably cut everyone's hair in the neighborhood (R.I.P Q), my afro had grown so tall and nappy, by this point, there was no way I would be able to get it looking right before school. In a panic, I ran downstairs and told my mom's boyfriend, Tony, the situation concerning my appearance, and my hair.

He said, "Well, the clothes don't look too bad (side eye). I mean the white shirt is definitely bringing the outfit together."

As he looked over my outfit, I'm thinking to myself, "Nigga, just shoot me."

Then, raising an eyebrow, Tony looked up at my hair.

"I only have a few minutes before the bus comes. What can I do with my hair?" I begged him.

"Come on," he said, as I followed him towards the kitchen.

Turning on the front stove burner, and reaching in the kitchen junk drawer, Tony grabbed a black metal comb-looking object, and placed it on the open flame for about five minutes - until the comb was smoking with a strong burnt smell. He grabbed a kitchen chair and said, "sit down." I felt as if I was about to go under the knife. (I later learned that this mystery object was called a "hot comb" or "straightening comb," it was very popular in the 70s and 80s within the African American community.)

Tony then took the hot-comb, and slowly placed it on the top right side of my afro, combing it over to the left side of my head. I felt the heat from the comb just slightly on my scalp. I worried that if he pressed just a little bit harder, my scalp would receive first, second, or third degree burns for sure.

He then went back to the top right again to start over, but this time, he combed downward in the opposite direction forming a wide part at the top right of my head - a *side part*.

Finally, he grabbed a jar of hair grease out the drawer; opened it; placed two fingers inside, grabbing out a heaping glob; rubbed it into the palm of his hands; and applied the hair grease - *heavily*. My once-tall afro was now a slicked down, steamed and pressed, Sammy Davis, Jr. special, looking as if I was about to throw on some tap dance shoes to perform in a hot Las Vegas show.

Suddenly, the bus pulled up, and me, with my nine-year-old hair looking like Sammy Davis Jr., knew I was about to be destroyed and devastated by the kids at school.

The moment I reached the top of the bus steps, the kids lost it; I hadn't heard kids laugh that loud at a circus. I, *somehow*, made my way to my seat through all the finger pointing and laughter.

The day only got worse.

When I arrived at school, I had to climb a flight of stairs to get to my homeroom. Every morning, two homeroom teachers stood at the top of the steps to greet the students.

Well, that day, when I walked up the steps, the two teachers saw me, the red and white checkered pants, the white shirt and the Sammy Davis Jr. hair. *They* couldn't even hold in their laughter.

I was crushed, and I still had picture day ahead of me. I was embarrassed, and at this point, there was absolutely nothing I could do about it. The day crept by. Around noon, I arrived at the auditorium. Students were already there with their classes standing in line getting ready for pictures and we were up next.

It was my turn up, and the photographer was really nice. She made sure I was sitting straight and ready for the picture. She then went behind the camera, under a black cloth, and before snapping the picture, from underneath the cloth, she said, "Alright now, give me a big smile."

"I am smiling." I replied.

She stuck her head out the cloth and said, "Well, you don't want to just take the picture like that."

"Well, I *am* smiling," I rebutted, maintaining my version of a smile.

"No, that's not a smile. You just have your teeth kinda hanging out your mouth, and you don't want to take it like that," she said.

My little heart was devastated.

The truth of the matter is, I didn't know how to smile because I never wanted to show my teeth.

I know, I know, I tried to warn you about this story, and trust me it's still a bit challenging to tell. However, I wanted to share that because you would be amazed at how many people are being held back by incidents that happened to them as a child. This is so serious, and I could have easily gone in a shell or hid under a rock somewhere, and never even tried to win; but, that voice inside me kept reminding my heart and mind that I AM somebody. I had a deep passion to succeed, and I knew that my gifts and talents were not for me to waste, but to use to the best of my ability. This was the key for me getting out of poverty, and away from the location where I was raised, all so I could give myself an opportunity to experience a better quality of life.

Now that I'm older, and make pretty good money, I try to keep my appearance up from top to bottom, and as you may have guessed by now, no one can't shut me up. All I want to do is talk, smile and take tons of pictures. I'm sure the followers on my social media pages are like, "Wow, he sure takes a whole lot of pictures." Well, that's because they have no idea of my story - until now.

I realize that everyone has a past of some sort. Some may be very dark moments or events that have shaped their lives, but do we let that hold us back? Do we just give up or have a lifelong pity-party? NO! Of course not....

We reflect and move on to the next.

We must enter into what I call a, "MIND SET GO" state. We set our minds, and go forth, knowing that once your MIND is SET, it's time to GO! In other words, move forward into action and execute change.

I've read many books and heard many people say: "Let go of your past." While you do need to loosen your grip on the past, or rather, loosen the grip it has on you - your past is important. Take for instance, growing a plant. You start by planting a seed. The seed gets buried in the earth. The seed begins to germinate. It sprouts out of the dark place where no one can see. It begins to grow upward, and suddenly, breaks through the ground where photosynthesis takes place.

While the plant lives in the light, the plant still needs its connection to the earth for gaining nutrients and stability.

The story about my childhood keeps me stable and humble, it helps me to remember where I came from, and how I made it through, when others may have given up. Yes, it was sad and cloudy, but I knew there was light on the outside of what I was dealing with.

Listen, I don't have to get deep or scientific to get you to understand this analogy; however, we are all like seeds planted in the earth: we are striving to grow, to move upward towards answers, towards truth, in search of knowledge and enlightenment, and the best part about it is...

LIFE AND THE UNIVERSE ARE ON OUR SIDE TO HELP US.

We're all familiar with the phrase: "everything in life happens for a reason." Your past may seem a little dark and dirty, but don't drown yourself in self-pity, or allow your dark times to hold you back. Instead, use it, let it motivate you. Position your "Mind Set Go" attitude to break through your tough moments; which are only there to keep you stable and grounded, and to strengthen and nurture you, just as the dirt does for the plant. People ask me all the time: "How did you make it? Who did you look up to?" I simply tell them, "I just wanted to WIN!"

Trust me, I've seen some very challenging days, times in which I felt like, *what's the use*. However, I would see others making it both in person and on television. I saw others becoming successful and walking in their purpose. That's when I decided to, not only change my thinking, but to translate it into action. Once my Mind was Set, it was time to GO, learning that we are all much Bigger than we know.

Right now, you have to start taking the right paths and walking in it. This is one of the top reasons this book was written: to help you dig deep into your souls' files, grabbing your unanswered questions and unspoken desires, and launching them into your life for your purpose.

I never had a role model growing up;

I just had people I didn't want to be like

A few years ago, I was in a meeting with three owners of a particular business, along with their lawyer. We were having a discussion about bringing me in as one of their partners. Needless to say, I was happy to be there, and honored for the opportunity to potentially join these awesome ladies in business.

The three women had been in business for years, and were looking to modernize their company, with hopes of taking it to the next level by gaining more youth. Now, the meeting went well. We discussed all the details about duties and who would be responsible for what; however, near the end of the meeting, one of the owners slowly put her hand up and begin to ask the lawyer a question.

She asked, "After going over everything and hearing all the details, what is your take on us merging together? I mean as a professional, what do you feel?"

The lawyer folded her hands on the table with a pleasant smile and said, "I feel after hearing everything, this is a great idea. I feel your business would be in good hands with this young man. I can tell he is the type of young man that, when he wants something to succeed, he will let nothing stand in his way."

The ladies began to smile as if they felt the same way, which, of course, caused me to smile. Removing her glasses, the lawyer looked over at me, with a serious, yet pleasant look on her face; it was as if she was a mother talking to her son about life. She looked me straight in the eyes, (you know the look someone gives you to make sure you hear them clearly, making sure it gets deep down in your spirit, yeah, well, that's exactly how it was) and then spoke the following into my world:

"Young man you have a glow about you, a light in your eyes I haven't seen in a long time. Now hear me good. The world can be a very dark place at times, and it will try everything in its power to put your light out. Don't let them do It!"

That moment changed my whole mindset. She made me feel I had something valuable within myself that I needed to protect, and more importantly, *use*. We all have that constant inner voice reminding us that we are bigger than we know, and every now and then, someone else also sees it. When it's acknowledged, it's time to SET your Mind and GO! It may be a moment when you're at work, sitting at your desk, and the CEO comes in and ask for you, *specifically*, to work on a project. They aren't looking at you as just a low-level employee, they see someone with value, and have taken an interest in helping you to realize you can become more!

Or, it may be a clash you have with friends, or even family, in your circle. Their lives are stagnant, they are content and relaxed, but you know there is more to life. Have you ever had a friend or know someone stuck in their same-old-same-old routine? Their spark is gone, and it appears they have lost all fight within themselves. Part of you becomes distant; you don't want them rubbing off on you now that you realize the power of your drive. You have become this fighter that not only believes, but knows, you are on this earth for a reason; and for you, there is no stopping until you are in your proper place, position, and calling. Trust me when I say, be very mindful of all the company you keep. Surround yourself with go-getters, like-minded people who are driven and focused, like you. We all are puzzle pieces to an amazing master-piece called Life, and there is an urgency of "Now" to get into your designated position. Your true life depends on it, and trust me, I am only touching the tip of the iceberg when talking about this masterpiece puzzle. We will revisit this again as we move forward.

-The biggest risk in life, is not taking a risk.

Chapter Two

Time Currency

If you ask someone right now, "what are your goals in life?" they would probably give an answer like: "to buy a house; buy a new a car; land a good job; gain fame; have a fortune; become popular," etc. These are all good responses. However, if you had asked what is *important* to them, some of these answers would make the list, sure, but not all of them. Most of the time, when we talk about what's important to us we say things like family, money, religion, health or love. However, we rarely mention one of the most important assets in our lives: time.

Time, and what you do with it, is the foundation for reaching your goals. Michael Jordan is arguably the greatest basketball player of all times. He said that "if you put in that work, results will come" I love this quote, and when I read it I became more focused on what I was doing with my time, realizing I must put in that work.

In order to put the work in, I am required to use the power and the gift of time. This may seem like a simple task, that is until you start investigating and documenting what you are doing with your time. Sadly to say, many would find ourselves wasting our TIME on things that do not help us reach our goals.

Millionaires are Millionaires because they have MONEY.

Most of the time, if it wasn't already passed down, they have INVESTED, spending their money on good INVESTMENTS (i.e. things that bring a positive return like real estate, stocks bonds, or insurance). If you happened to know millionaires, pay attention. It is rare you'll ever see them spending money on things that fail to give them a positive return, or on items I like to call...

Bullshit.

A millionaire's money is as valuable to them as your paycheck is to you. Even if some money is lost, many times, they know the proper investment to get it back.

Time, on the other hand, is not that easy to get back. Once it's lost - it's gone forever. Time is your most valuable asset. Change your thinking, start investing your time in things that will ultimately give you a positive return. First, ask yourself what are you spending your time on? Is it that job you dread getting up early for every morning, only to feel unappreciated? Is it television shows? Social Media? A bad relationship? A Toxic friendship?

Now, I am not saying that "some" of these things should be completely eliminated out of your life. I am simply saying, be mindful and aggressive, and stop investing so much of your valuable asset in some of those things. Simply put - stop wasting your TIME.

Once you start to learn the importance of YOU and your VALUE, then, and only then, will you start to position yourself on a better vibration, better surroundings and in much better circumstances. So, why haven't you positioned yourself yet? That's easy: you haven't grasped the fact that YOU'RE BIGGER THAN YOU KNOW. However, that's beginning to CHANGE!

Often, I've been asked if I would ever write a self-help book. I always laugh when I hear that question. My thought on it was this: there are millions of "Self Help" books out there. However, I couldn't seem to find that many "Self-Know" books. In my opinion, I think it's much more important to "know" yourself, before you can honestly help yourself. For example, it would be pretty hard for a doctor to give medicine without first knowing the patient or the patient's symptoms. They must first get to know their patient and what's going on with them in order to help them.

One of my goals for this book is to get you to challenge your thinking, and influence you to start listening to the inner you. The real you is constantly trying to lead and guide you into truth - not what you've been taught or emotionally driven by. You are here to succeed in life, with a greater purpose that even YOU haven't fully figured out yet. However, realize now that you have all the tools you need to complete the task.

Up until now, you may or may not have focused much on what you've been doing with your time. However, I'm pretty sure by now you realize that time is currency, and it needs to be spent on things that matter. One of the most important ways you can find out how BIG you really are, is when you gain the consciousness, discipline, and power to spend your TIME wisely. You will begin to gain a positive return, advancing you forward towards your goals, your visions, and, more importantly, your purpose - in a *timely* fashion.

In today's world of technology, and of course the ever-growing world of social media, becoming easily distracted and taken off course is almost inevitable. While technology and social media are useful, it is important not to get too caught up and deviate from your course.

In finding out that you're "Bigger Than YOU know," you must realize that you are also bigger than the objects and desires that surround you. We tend to put our desire for the material above our journey. While material objects can be useful and enjoyable, it is your job to make sure they don't become, "TIME CURRENCY WASTERS," taking you off the journey to your purpose.

Naturally, we all have moments when we put "things" before ourselves. However, once you enter into the space of enlightenment, these possessions will become minor, and you'll spend less of your "TIME CURRENCY" on them. Realize that you are on the road to greatness, a fulfilling life of prosperity, joy and purpose - ON YOUR OWN TERMS. Not because someone has taught you or used a fear tactics trying to focus you. Let your reason be that you are tired of the feeling that keeps reminding you...

"YOU SHOULD BE DOING MORE WITH YOUR LIFE, BEING MORE AND BECOMING MORE."

You have talents and innate abilities you haven't shared with anyone. Ask yourself, "how long will you sit back and watch others move forward obtaining the things you desire?" Over and over again, you think to yourself, "I can do that, and maybe even better." Instead of just sitting there, hoping, "STIR UP THE GIFT THAT'S IN YOU!"

Let me make this clear for you. If you are making a fresh pitcher of lemonade (yes, not the artificial powder kind) you would start by filling a pitcher with water. Next, you'd take some fresh, ripe, lemons, cut them up, and squeeze them into the pitcher. After that, you would add the sugar. NOW STOP! At this very moment, you have EVERYTHING you need to make a good pitcher of lemonade. Right? Everything is inside the pitcher, at full capacity, ready and fully capable of producing results for its purpose - AWESOME!! Now taste it. *What happened???* It's BITTER! *Why?*

It's simple, *you haven't stirred it up yet!* I am telling you right now...

DO NOT LET YOU GIFTS, YOUR TALENTS, YOUR CALLING OR YOUR PURPOSE, FALL DORMANT AT THE BOTTOM - STIR IT UP!

Stop wasting your TIME CURRENCY on things and people that don't matter. Instead, STIR IT UP! Never forget: you are Bigger than YOU know, and now that your MIND is SET, it's time to GO!

There is another form of Time that affects us all, whether we recognize it or not. A couple of years ago my wife and I decided to purchase our second home. Our kids were getting older, and we felt we could use more space, so we started the process. We searched for houses in areas we wanted to live, the style of house we wanted, and the things we wanted in it: design, bath, closet space, room counts, etc.

After finding the house we wanted, we posted an 8 1/12 x 11 sheet of paper on the wall by our bed of the home's interior and exterior diagram, with the word "attraction" written underneath. We did this so we could wake up every morning and see our home.

Now, for those who have gone through the process of buying a new home, you already know it can be a ROLLERCOASTER! Ups and downs, twists and turns, the normal hurry up and wait process, and for us, it was absolutely no different.

In 2008, as you probably know, there was a major real estate market meltdown. It was a mess, and some are still suffering from it. The housing market balloon popped as a result of so many mortgages falling through; this was the residual effect of people obtaining loans they couldn't afford.

So did this affect me? Of course it did. The crash caused a lot of lenders to begin examining applicants under a microscope; making sure we jumped through hoops, cut cleanly through the red tape, all while crossing every fine line, for a loan approval.

By the time we received our approval, my wife started working full-time, helping us to save towards a down payment, along with settlement cost. Our minds were made up, we knew what we wanted, and we knew we were ready. That's when we started to notice happenings and events taking place - *in our favor.* It was as if we had shared with the world about us buying a new home, people starting inquiring about our process right out of the blue.

My business started to grow, and every person we needed to make this deal go through suddenly started to show up. A new accountant replaced my old accountant. Next, a realtor called me saying someone told her to call us about purchasing a new home. However, when she called, she was already locked in my phone from a few years back, but we never met. From each of those coincidental events, I had to pause and realize, WE WERE TAPPED IN! Tapped into what, you say? Tapped into "DIVINE TIME."

Divine Time: An unexplainable zone or space. A spiritual force with power and unlimited divine consciousness and intelligence to control or maneuver, anything, anybody, anywhere without permission. It conspires and intervenes, spiritually, with the Universe on your behalf, so that you may obtain the things you want/need, that is not in your control to obtain spiritually, or even naturally, for your purpose.

After realizing I was not alone on this journey, or any journey for that matter, I decided to pay attention, watch, investigate; and surrendered to being led by a force working in my favor that was much bigger than me. It was unseen, but there, causing each situation to iron out, allowing people to show up in places I needed them to be that normally wouldn't have been there, maneuvering and shifting things in my favor as if my thoughts and intentions were being heard.

On a Monday morning, I received an unexpected email from my loan officer asking to take a check to the IRS to get it stamped: it was one of the last things we needed to do for us to close on our new home.

Normally, this wouldn't have been a problem; however, it was 10 a.m. and I had a very important meeting to attend at 11:30 a.m., so I figured, if I leave now I could make it downtown to the IRS, then head to the loan office with the stamped check, leaving just enough time to make it to my meeting at 11:30 a.m.

Finally, I made it to the IRS building, jumped on the elevator to the third floor and proceeded down the hallway toward the Internal Revenue Service Room. There were people outside the door standing around and even sitting on the floor, all with that look as if they knew they were going to be there for hours!

I walked past the line of people outside of the office, got inside, and every seat in there was filled - which explained the line outside. I thought to myself, "YOU GOTTA BE KIDDING ME!" However, it was tax season. Feeling discouraged I thought, "Well I'm here now," so I went over to the counter where they had a ticket number machine. I pressed the button for my ticket and the number 401 came out. I looked at the number board to see what number they were on, it said: 195 (I almost laughed out loud). I mean, could things get any worse?

I turned and looked at all the people in back of me, and to my surprise, there was a seat in the second row behind this gentleman who looked familiar, but I couldn't figure out why or even his name. Anyway, I needed to get this check stamped, so I had to accept the fact that I was going to be here for a while.

I pulled out my phone to send a text message to the people I was meeting with notifying them, unfortunately, I was not going to make the meeting. Right before I hit "send," the familiar gentlemen that sat in front of me stands up, looks me in the face, reaches his hands out to shake my hand and says, "Alright D I'm outta here I can't wait here all day."

I reached out to shake his hand and said, "Ok bro." Now again, I didn't know this gentleman; however, I was used to people knowing who I was because of my many different professions, and the fact my name is very popular in my hometown area. We shook hands, and I felt a small, balled up, piece of paper pressed into my hand from his. I look at him, and he looks at me in the eyes as if I could hear him saying, "you are all good to go."

We shook hands, and he walked out of the office area. I looked down at what was left in my hand: the balled-up piece of paper. Slowly I opened it. It was his ticket, with the number 201 on it. I then looked up at the number board again, and they were on number 198. I smiled so hard inside and out in disbelief! What looked like hours of waiting and a canceled meeting became a 10-minute wait. GOD IS GOOD!

I texted my wife while sitting there about what just happened. Now, my wife is a big numbers person and astrology reader, so after receiving my text she looked up the number 201, and then she returned a text of the meaning of the number.

It said...

"Angel number 201 is a message that things will be going in your desired direction, and wonderful new opportunities will present themselves when the timing is right. Maintain faith and trust, knowing that your angels and the Universe are fully supporting you in every way."

I was done! Blown away, as this was more confirmation that I was indeed operating on Divine Time, which was indeed working in my favor! I texted my wife back "WOW" and the fact that I only wish I knew the gentlemen, so I could thank him for what he did for me at the IRS office.

Three days later, I was at my place of business. I received a call from my cleaning crew to give me an update and remind me of what supplies were needed, so I planned on heading to Home Depot. Home Depot closed at 10 p.m., it was currently 9:15 p.m., which was not a big deal since I was, literally, 10 minutes away. I finished up what I was doing, arrived at Home Depot around 9:30 p.m. and began to look for the cleaning supplies.

I had a hard time finding one item, so I asked one of the employees if they could show me it's location. She directed me to go way to the back of aisle number 25 and said, "there should be someone back there that can help you."

I went to the back and found another employee in the commercial cleaning department. I said, "Excuse me, I'm trying to find a product for the restrooms at my business." He said, "Oh sure..." As he began to tell me where to go, I heard another voice in the back of me yelling out, "HEY, how did you make out with that the other day?" I turned around and guess who it was? You got it! It was the guy from the IRS office that gave me the ticket number 201! I was shocked!

I smiled so hard, and immediately walked over to him with my hand already out and said, "I want to THANK YOU so much for what you did for me at the IRS office. You have no idea how much you helped me out."

He said, "Yeah man, I don't even know why I came there that day, I already knew they couldn't help me, so I just left".

I was in awe! Everything worked out in perfect timing: "DIVINE TIME." I was even able to Thank the gentlemen for helping me out, after telling my wife I only wish I could thank him!

How does one Tap into Divine Time? It's simple: you have to make a Conscious Internal Commitment (CIC) to move forward toward your purpose, using your gifts and talents.

-You must agree with GOD and cooperate with the Universe.

That thing that keeps pulling you, inspiring you to move forward, to elevate and causes you to grow? That is God's gift, given to you, that wasn't taught, but can be executed by you naturally, like no one else can. Then, the Universe will conspire, and come into agreement with you to make sure you obtain the things you want/need on your journey in life.

One week later, we moved into our Dream Home. Our address is 1122, which means, "New beginnings, accomplishment, peace and foundation, balance and harmony." Oh, I can't make this stuff up.

For years, I told my wife that even though my life was filled with family and friends, I felt alone. What I didn't understand was time: time currency, personal time, and Divine time. Once I discovered time, every element my life started falling into place and I didn't feel so alone anymore. I've come to realize We Don't have TIME - To Waste TIME!

Chapter Three

Pure Passion Power

Music! I absolutely love music, ALL kinds of music, and everything from the studio to the radio and concerts. Have you ever seen Michael Jackson perform? He was mesmerizing: From the singing to him gliding across the stage as if he was truly on the moon or walking on air.

How about the voice of Ms. Celine Dion? Remember the theme song from the Mega Hit movie Titanic? When she sings those classic words "Near, far, wherever you are I believe that the heart does go on." Whether you hear it, sing it and even while typing the lyrics, you can still feel it deep inside your spirit, and with that strong emotional drive that enhances her delivery - simply Amazing.

When we get the privilege to experience these gifted people, who have, individually, touched the world, you can't help but wonder what makes them different. What makes them able to reach that pinnacle in their life?

Was it hard work and dedication? I'm sure it wasn't easy, and took a lot of sacrifices; however, if you pay close attention and listen a little deeper, you can hear and see the secret ingredient that separates them from the average, and that is PURE PASSION POWER, or the three P's, as I I like call it. They have all developed into the outliers of their profession, and ultimately, into the Superstars they are.

If there is any, one, attribute that I may use to describe what makes success possible, I would have to say without a shadow of a doubt, PASSION. Passion is a strong, and at times, unbearable emotion. It is a strong enthusiasm or excitement for something - a must-have. Passion is the fuel for all your dreams and visions, and we all have it however, most are unaware of its need and power. Anybody can do a good job, but it is the ones that are passionate, that stand out and reach even higher heights.

Have you ever found yourself doing things, or being a part of something, or maybe even working at a job you just weren't connected to? How about a relationship you've spent time and years in, knowing you deserve better, wanting more, knowing you could be experiencing a better quality of life? You feel stuck, because deep inside, you know better. I'll say this: you're not the first and surely won't be the last. One day I was headed to work and the thought came to mind…

"Why aren't you doing the things you Love?"

My ambition was there, and my desire was strong; I always felt inside I could/should be doing more. I have the gifts, the talent and the intelligence to make it happen - so what's the problem? I'll tell you what my problem was, and it could very well be yours: I had a FEAR of facing the responsibility of TOTAL CHANGE.

Now, this may not be the primary reason for not entering into a MIND SET GO state, and moving forward, towards your purpose. It may not be the main reason for not using your PASSION power. However, most of the time, FEAR is the root and the answer to why you are still forfeiting your life, settling, and continually wearing a mask. Fear is acting out a character that's hiding the real you and all the Awesome potential you possess.

We all know that fear can come in many forms. We're not talking about healthy fears: fire, angry dogs, your mother-in-law... NO, we are talking about Fear of what people may think, the fear of new territory, different places, the fear of losing friends that can't accept the real you or a better you.

You cower in fear at the unknown, at people judging you, at people thinking you're better than them. These are the most common fear barriers that will keep you from moving forward. DON'T LET IT. Let your PURE PASSION POWER TAKE OVER, and trust it.

Passion is more than a feeling, it is a CONTAGIOUS power: a deep strong emotion that we all have. Pure Passion Power is like a strong magnet to whatever it's near. A singer on stage has passion. A sports figure on the field, or even a school teacher teaching history to young students, all have passion. This is what they love to do. This is what they live to do.

Your passion and purpose are like two magnets. Your passion is reaching out beyond you, and your purpose is pulling you towards it. What a wonderful connection! How long will you fight the pull for your purpose? How long will you allow yourself to be a person or people pleaser?

I had to ask myself these same questions. But then I realized I was sick of hearing those three ugly words in my head: Coulda, Shoulda, Woulda. "Oh, HELL NAW!" I say. Using the gifts and talents you've been blessed with, it's time to SET your Mind, and GO! Once you add the secret ingredient of Pure Passion Power, you will make it happen.

- You Must become an Enemy to Average

Listen clearly, Champions are not Champions from being just average people. They are not selling millions of dollars' worth of products because the products are average. People that make it big on television did not make it there being average. An enemy of average means that average thinkers will always clash with you. They won't understand your moves in life - personal or business. They will try to say and do things that discourage you, or keep you from pursuing and accomplishing your goals.

- Your passion must be fuel for your dreams and visions

You must have it: that energy, that love, that determination, to go get what you're after. Once you obtain that energy, that passion, share it, so it can multiply. I learned a long time ago that I was a person of surplus. I always strive to have extra, or simply, more than enough. Never allow others to make you feel guilty for having extra, or wanting more. Most of the things in life that we love, naturally, we want more of it.

I hear people say all the time, "less is more." Well, that depends on what we're talking about. I'm sure you would agree that less food wouldn't be more; or less space wouldn't be more; and of course, ladies, fewer shoes and clothes, definitely, do not fit in this phrase. I've also found that the people that say less is more, often times don't want better. Chances are, they don't know better because they haven't experienced better. These types of people are usually, small-minded thinkers, and most likely, tried before and have given up.

When my children come to me with their ideas, I always smile. I want to know how bad they want it, how deep is their desire to achieve it, and what's their plan to get it.

I was once told that, "everything in life has a price, find out the price, and pay it." I tell my children this all the time: what are you willing to pay? Are you willing to pay the price of giving up your time or something close to you? Are you willing to sell something valuable to you, to gain money to fund your new idea? Or are you willing to let go of a habit you love so much, to fill that space with your new adventure?

I laugh because, it may seem like a bit much, but this is the only way you can truly find out how passionate you are about something, and it's not just an impulse. YOU MUST WANT IT BAD!!

Listen, I can't stress enough how Pure Passion Power is the secret ingredient to, literally, everything that has a need to advance. It is your fuel, and you will not get very far without it.

By all means, the information I am sharing with you is NOT easy. There are challenges and sacrifices involved, of course. Some of us are not in the position to just up and leave a job. Some have families that depend on them financially. Trust me, I get it, and you're not the only one in this predicament. Chances are, like many of us, you're getting older and your gifts and talents have grown. What you thought you loved doing has changed, your desires have even changed, as well as your tolerance.

Now that the seeds of your gifts and talents have blossomed and shown themselves, you're probably thinking, "WOW I need to pursue this, it's my real passion and I didn't even know it till now."

The only problem is you may be tied into a few things (previously mentioned), that are preventing you from pursuing your true passion and what you were born to do - to live out your purpose. So what do you do? You start your passion in the form of a hobby. By taking a little time and spending it on doing what you love. Not only will this get you on the path of finally pursuing your purpose, it will bring you fulfillment, it will balance things out for you and also be therapeutic. It's never too late to jump on the path of your purpose.

Mind Set Go also means to prepare yourself, to draw the right things to you. Well, Mr. Reed, that's just it, "I can't seem to draw the right things to me, I'm focused on my goals etc..."

If this is you, then let me say this....

Check your BAIT!

Listen, if you and I went on a fishing trip, we would look a little crazy standing inside the boat, focusing on the fish in the ocean, hoping, sooner or later, we would catch the fish by doing nothing else. The moment we set our goal, and decided to go out to catch some fish, we should have moved on to the second part: determining, *how* we will achieve that goal. I say, we go straight to our "BAIT".

If you're ever at the point where things aren't being drawn to you, and you can't seem to find yourself in the right positions, you must CHECK YOUR BAIT. What are you adding to your rod that causes you to attract the right things, and what are you adding to your rod that's causing you to attract the wrong things?

Is your Bait right? Do you even have Bait? What are you trying to draw from? I swear, I think I just heard all millions of you reading this book say, "MONEY!" Now, that's PURE PASSION POWER!!

Again, hard work is AWESOME and will definitely put you in the Mind Set Go state of chasing money, which is okay. However,...

Quality and Consistency will have MONEY chasing you.

I added a post on my social sites for one of my businesses saying, "we are not trying to be the best; Our goal is Quality and Consistency." I wrote that because I understand that being the best is a limited position. What I mean by "limited position," is sooner or later someone else may, and will, come along and take the top spot. However, when it comes down to you adding that Pure Passion Power to your work habits, and the time you spend working on a project or craft to deliver quality, you can't help but draw the right things to you. Pure Passion Power - we do this because we LOVE IT!

Chapter Four

Believing Is Deceiving

JUNE 18, 2013, NBA Finals, Miami Heat vs San Antonio Spurs; it was game 6, the score: Spurs 95 and Miami 92 with 19.5 seconds on the clock. The Crowd was going WILD! Dwayne Wade brings the ball up, as the clock ticks down he moves left, almost getting trapped in the corner by the defense.

LeBron James shakes his man, and quickly moves to the top left of the key, Wade sees him. Wade jumps and passes the ball over his defender's head, and into the hands of LeBron James, he catches, jumps and shoots with 11 seconds on the clock... HE MISSES!

Chris Bosh quickly grabs the rebound, kicks it out to Ray Allen in the bottom right-hand corner, with 7 seconds on the clock left, he steps back behind the three-point line - he shoots!! BANG!! ALL NET! Ray Allen ties the game up with five seconds left on the clock sending the game into OVERTIME!

WOW! As a sports fan, who could forget this historical moment? Needless to say, I was always a Ray Allen fan, and wasn't surprised when he hit the big shot. He's practically been successful in hitting this shot his whole career, which leads me to why I even started this chapter off this way.

Like millions of people around the world, I was glued to the T.V. Although the Miami Heat eventually won in overtime, there was a moment after the game that was an even bigger moment for me, and it actually altered my thinking on how I view and approach things today. At the end of the game, a reporter caught up with Ray Allen for his postgame remarks.

The reporter said, "I am here with Ray Allen who hit one of the biggest shots of his career sending a game six into overtime." She asked, "Ray, how did you feel once the ball got into your hands, what was it like, what were your thoughts?"

Ray Allen, without a shadow of a doubt said, "I Knew I would make it. Some things in life you just know, and to me that's every bit of the mindset you need when out here on the floor".

PAUSE!!!! (Think for five seconds)

Now, this may not mean much to some people, but for me, WOW! His statement, to me, was bigger than the shot he made in the game. My focus changed, as well as my perspective. I didn't want to just believe I could make it happen anymore, I wanted to "KNOW" I could.

ALL my life I've been taught to believe in something: believe in yourself, believe in this type of religion, believe you can make it. All of this is ok to me; however, "KNOWING" launched me into a new space, a new energy, on a whole different vibration.

I felt surer of myself, and more confident, as if I had awakened the true me inside. In that moment I said, "That's it! I'm going to start 'knowing' and stop limiting myself to just belief or 'believing.'"

I even looked up the definition of the word believe. It means: to accept something as being true. Now, that doesn't't *make* it true. It just means you are accepting it, rather you have facts or not, no further explanation needed.

If someone told you right now, that at the end of the today "they believe" they're going to give you ten thousand dollars, you probably would be extremely happy and overjoyed. Now, on the other hand, what if that same per-son said, "at the end of the day I know I'm going to give you ten thousand dollars."

This becomes a game changer. Your extreme excitement and overjoyed feeling just skyrocketed into a place of certainty and security that this was going to happen, with absolutely no doubt. This is exactly how you should feel about everything you put your mind to in life.

- You can't elevate until you eliminate your limitations.

There are some people that think inside the box, and there are some that think outside the box. Then, there are people who ask the question, "What Box?" These are the people who are limitless. To some, this may sound impossible, but that's only because of the limits you put on yourself or allow others to put on you. Okay, sure, if you want to outrun a car, or fly off a building without a plane, yes, that would be considered *out of reason*. However, the mental, or even outside limitations, that constantly tell you, you can't do something, because of X Y and Z, will prevent you from elevating into your purpose.

This may rattle your thinking, but STOP BELIEVING you can't make it and STOP BELIEVING you CAN make it! Yes, you heard me correctly I said: "CAN MAKE IT." Get your Mind Set on KNOWING you can make it happen; *knowing* you can be truly happy; *knowing* you can be successful; *knowing* you can be what you desire to be and called to be without regrets; *knowing* that even your true life partner or significant other is out there somewhere waiting on you, as well, to collaborate with you in pursuing your purpose. Now, is there a time to believe? Of course, there is. I am not saying we have to take believing off the table, absolutely not. What I am saying is, when it comes to believing something, it should be given as a credit, based on experience, proof, or validation that may have been shown in the past. Believing can be deceiving, especially if you're are not willing to investigate for knowledge, which, will lead you to the truth. This again will not be an easy transition, going from believing to knowing, and trust me, some things you may never know, and that's fine, there is peace found in that as well. If something is vital to you, and connected to your purpose, it shall be revealed, or shall I say, "Known."

In every journey, there is always a process. It includes taking small steps of getting yourself out of anything, that may be holding you back from your visions and goals. We must plan our escape from our old ways of thinking. Yes, you must plan to escape from your old mindset to capture your NEW MINDSET, then after that, it's time for a daily practice of "Embracing Change."

One simple thing a lot of people fail to realize is: Change, requires Change! That's right. Everything that doesn't contribute to the advancement of fulfilling your purpose, has to be done away with first. I don't want to make this sound easy, in fact, it is very challenging, but it can be accomplished, once you have allowed yourself to enter into a MIND SET GO state.

Embrace change

It may be simple for some, but this obstacle can be the most difficult to conquer for most of us.

Change is a must - period! Without it, we can't grow. It's just that simple. Progress, Success, Elevation, all have to come through the windows of change. For most of us, we have to get it the old fashion way, and that is changing our MINDSET and GO.

In today's world of the internet and social media, you no longer have to believe in just anything. If you don't know something, just type it in, and you can find the information in seconds. Knowledge will always be power, but AGAIN, it is more important to…

Know yourself first, before you can help yourself.

I say, it's time to start knowing the fact that you are on your way. Don't be deceived by that voice constantly trying to persuade you that it's ok to just believe, but rather, be enlightened and challenge yourself to Know and Grow.

The first step to challenging yourself is to be honest with yourself. Don't be deceived by what you simply believe. You have to recognize your strong, and weak, points.

Learn your strong attributes, so you can then capitalize on them. Learn your weak points, so you may recognize them and prevent them from hindering meeting your goals and purpose.

Secondly, you want to gather all your resources, and start working on gathering all the information you need to get yourself moving towards your purpose. What hobbies are you interested in? What craft constantly pulls your attention? What career do you feel is a perfect fit for you? What is something you always had a desire for?

Research and learn about it, investigate each of them, get to know the ins and outs until it becomes embedded in you, and go for it. Again, Set your Mind, and Go.

Third, you want to network! If you don't network, you won't work. Start being around like-minded people who share your desire and vision. Check your ego at the door, and start being around people that are simply just smarter than you, or who have already traveled the same road you're starting on.

There is an old saying - iron sharpens iron. However, first, you have to be around the iron. Find some people who are driven and focused, learn from them, ask questions and see what paths they all took to get where they are today.

Needless to say, I'm a fairly good speaker. I love to motivate and bring people closer to their calling. I see the big picture of their lives in ways they miss. I don't just know I possess this talent, I use it, I work at it. I watch and listen to Motivating Powerhouses such as, TD Jakes, Les Brown, Tony Robbins, Zig Ziglar, Steve Jobs and, of course, Barack Obama.

These gentlemen deliver their messages and speeches with power and inspiration that infiltrates your soul to the core. Just talking about it now gets me ready to take off running. That's exactly the type of feeling and energy you're going to need to stay motivated, and focused on your journey.

Never think you have to recreate the wheel. It's already laid out, in a pattern that somebody painstakingly created. Sure, you can add your own original twist, but the foundation is already laid: walk in it and perfect it - your way.

As you can see, I speak a lot about purpose. Other than your health, purpose is one of the most important things in your life. A life without purpose, is a life that exists without meaning.

What concerns me about the teaching of purpose, is that many people, feel they have to travel their path to purpose alone. While we each have our own purpose on earth, that doesn't't mean we don't share our purpose with others.

Let me explain, so you can see this more clearly. Say we are putting together a puzzle of someone riding a bike along a cemented pathway, that cuts through the grass, leading to a small bridge going over a small pond, on a blue-sky sunny day.

Now, the picture is usually on the front of the box. The first thing we all do is what? Yes, we drop all the pieces onto the table, then set up the box where we can see the picture of the puzzle. Then we begin sorting all the pieces out. At this point, we don't know exactly where all the pieces go; however, we start to match them up by color.

So, we take all the light blue pieces and group them together, because most likely, they will represent the blue sky. After that, we take all the brown puzzle pieces, and group them together to represent the bridge, and last we group all the green pieces together to represent the grass, and so on and so forth with the other pieces.

Ok, now that we have all of the pieces grouped together by color, the next thing we will do is to look at them. Let's start with the light blue ones first. Again, we don't know exactly where they all fit. However, we do know they all have the same PURPOSE - to create the sky of the puzzle.

We also have to realize every puzzle piece comes in different shapes and sizes, but again, they all serve the same "PURPOSE." Each blue piece might be placed in a predominantly different location, but they all serve the same PURPOSE - to fulfill the sky!

We will do the same thing with the other pieces. They too, serve in the PURPOSE of representing and fulfilling the bridge, and the grass, completing the whole puzzle, so it may be a solid, beautiful, piece of art.

We are just like the puzzle. *You are not alone*, and someone is doing, has done, or is about to do the very same thing you're doing, or about to do, concerning your purpose; they just might be in a different location on the puzzle, because they too have a purpose to fulfill.

Some people already started on this journey and can provide a blueprint for you in finding your purpose, revealing similar, or the same attributes as you, or, simply having something in common with your passion (i.e. they have already excelled in their purpose in life).

Some may not be as far as you are (that's if you've already found your purpose), and you will be the blueprint for them to follow. See, you are not alone. Yes, I repeat, it is very common for you to share the same purpose with someone else. I know what you've been taught, but this is the truth.

Trust me, I am not the only one in the world whose purpose is to inspire people. Many of us are called to the same purpose because we can't all reach the same people, at the same time.

Even when we look for a companion, it is important to find someone that understands and is compatible with your purpose. Understand, two peoples' purposes can clash. It is very challenging to have two people who are attracted to one another physically, or even spiritually, but have contradicting purposes in life.

For instance, what if a person's purpose in life is children, and their significant other just doesn't't have it in them to even deal with children?

Now, I am not saying it is impossible. However, it can be very challenging to coexist with someone who is not compatible with your purpose. Finding someone who understands, supports, and lines up with your purpose, or even has the same purpose as you have, is a beautiful thing.

Again, life is a masterpiece puzzle; however, it is not your job to find all the pieces. Rather, realize that you are one of the important pieces that are needed - and fit perfectly.

Over my life, I heard, over and over again, "if you believe more you can achieve more." Well, I beg to differ. If you believe more, you're taking the risk of being deceived more. Remember, you don't have to believe in anything that's real or anything that is real *to you*. All you have to do is KNOW it's real by gaining KNOWledge of it. With that knowledge, you'll begin to understand your purpose.

We have been programmed to BeLIEve and have BeLIEfs. Well, we can keep on BeLIEving, even without proof or results, but, all I ever saw was the "LIE" in the middle of these words.

I wanted to KNOW things, so I searched, until I found KNOWledge of the ONE, which is the beginning of understanding.

When you know better you grow better.

MIND SET GO!

Chapter Five

Too Close for Comfort

We all have differences: different upbringing, different cultures, lifestyles and of course different races. Out of all the difference we have, there are a few simple things that we do have in common.

We are all here on earth simply trying to experience a better quality of life.

I know that's pretty simple, but it's the truth. We all want better things in life, so we strive for them, whether it's for us personally, or for our loved ones.

A better quality of life doesn't't always have to mean a great big ole house on the hill, a fast fancy car, or that dream job you desire. A better quality of life to some people, could mean the freedom to come and go as you please; to travel and see the world, and the things in it; the freedom to be you; or it could simply mean a peace of mind doing the things you love.

On my own personal journey, as I've gotten older, I started to realize the importance and actions of LIFE. It is written in scriptures: "All things work together for the good." I had to ask myself, "What things?" and what does "All things" mean? Well, "ALL" means "Everything."

Everything is working in your favor. Once you've decided to walk fully in it, life has a way of working with everything (i.e. people, situations, things, circumstances, weather, you name it - All things) to get you on the right track to your purpose.

Before we go any further, let me make something very clear on my religious position. Am I religious? Absolutely not. Do I believe in GOD or a GOD? I always say, "You don't have to believe in whatever is real." So, NO I don't believe in GOD.

I absolutely KNOW THERE IS A GOD!

God is a being or a system that created us, and is Greater than us. I know there is nothing like it, him, or her. God is The Unknowable, The Almighty, The ONE.

I am well aware of the many spiritual books, such as, the Bible, (of course being raised Christian), the Quran, The Torah etc. All of which have awesome, profound teachings, proverbs, and scriptures that can be used to help and guide you on your own personal journey. However, I have evolved and come to realize that religion is not for me.

I wanted more: more understanding, the freedom to think on my own, without the influence of what others taught me to believe or think. I didn't like the control. I had questions; I wanted answers; and I knew they were out there.

I needed to be enlightened. I meditated; I observed; I studied; and I watched the Creator's Creations. The more I did, the more I learned about the Creator GOD. Again, this has nothing to do with any religious belief or affiliation, just mere personal experiences with a power and an energy much bigger than us all.

I was watching Steve Harvey on television one day, (if you don't know who Steve Harvey is by, now just google him. This successful man has about 14 jobs!) and during a commercial break, he was talking with the audience about being successful. He told them, "Every successful person that he knows had to take the jump. Not just any ole jump, but a conscious leap - without a net."

This was another life changing, WOW moment. There is a place we all love and are very familiar with; yet, it is very DANGEROUS. This place is called: "COMFORT." If we are not careful, we can get too comfortable with not doing, not being productive, or not enjoying our life to the fullest capacity. This includes everything from healthy exercise and healthier eating habits, to hobbies and career.

The reason comfort becomes so dangerous, is that it has the capability of hindering you from reaching your goals, and, most of all, your purpose.

You have to constantly remind yourself that you are too close to your goals to get comfortable. That's right: "TOO CLOSE FOR COMFORT." Now is not the time to fall asleep or remain in the trap of comfort a lot of us have fallen into.

I must say, Steve Harvey was keeping it real, and challenging us by helping us understand that comfort is not where it's at. You must be willing to become uncomfortable to succeed to the next level or the next phase of your life. Never neglect the fact that everything in life comes with a price, and as I said earlier, if you really want something bad enough, you will find out the cost and pay it.

Every now and then, I hear or see postings on social media concerning blessings saying, "GOD just opened a door for me." I guess doors being closed is the opposite, or at least that's how we think. The reason we have such a negative connotation with doors being closed, is because we see it as a failure or rejection. However, to the contrary, doors being closed is actually a good thing.

Some of us have fallen into the comfort zone simply because we've grown tired of doors closing on us, causing feelings of rejection and/or discouragement: I was supposed to have that job, but didn't get hired; I can't seem to find the right person for me; why can't I seem to get over this hump; another opportunity I was supposed to have failed on me... The list of closed doors goes on. And then - we settle.

Well, I am here to tell you to...

CHANGE YOUR PERSPECTIVE! Closed doors are for two reasons: PROTECTION and to CHANGE YOUR DIRECTION.

To protect you from the things unseen and unknown on the other side that may hinder you from fulfilling your purpose (i.e. situations, accidents, mishaps, people, relationships and even jobs). Instead of becoming discouraged when doors close in life, in the words of the great acapella song written by Mr. Bobby McFerrin, "Don't Worry Be Happy." It's only life conspiring to work things out in your favor.

When Changing your Direction, know that some doors shut in your life simply to wake you up, offering you the opportunity to be a part of something even greater.

Listen, if it's not working, it's not working for a reason. After you've done all you can to push through, to make it happen, and still no results...

DON'T GET DISCOURAGED!

Change your direction, even if it means going back to the beginning, or to your original plan.

Let's say you decided to try shooting a bow and arrow one day. You go out to a field, grab a target, set everything up, and then go several feet away from the target and prepare the bow for your shot. You grab an arrow, put it together with the bow, hold it up, and point it in the direction of your target - nothing happens. Why? Oh!! Of course! You didn't let go of the arrow correct? Yes, that's it! So you let go, and the arrow falls to the ground. Hmmm, what happened? I'll tell you what happened.

There are so many people who are failing to accept the fact that, when you are trying to hit the mark in your life, trying your best to grow, so you can score, requires some stretching and pulling. The reason why the arrow went straight to the ground, is that the shooter never PULLED BACK, which required some Stretching!!

I know, starting all over can be a BITCH sometimes, and having doors close on you is not a good feeling. However, just like the bow and arrow, some things require you to PULL BACK; this is so you can refocus yourself, with your eye square on the bullseye to add strength and accuracy to your delivery. Get this...you will hit your mark even faster.

Another thing to consider is this, on the low, we all want those hookups at the back door – the shortcuts in life. However, let me be the first to tell you, and learn this QUICK: in life, there are NO shortcuts. In finding your purpose, the shortcuts always turn out to be a long way.

So Remember:

- PULL BACK
- STRETCH YOURSELF
- REFOCUS
- LET GO
- BULLSEYE

Listen to life, and remember, you are TOO CLOSE FOR COMFORT. YES! Reminder: you are too close to your goals to get comfortable. You can still push and still move forward, but this time in a new direction. Once your MIND is SET, it's time to GO now, and MOVE FORWARD!

Chapter Six

Willingness to Win

There is an old saying, "If you don't have a plan for your life someone else will."

You may or may not realize it, but your life is your world. Your life should be your own. However, where you are right now, isn't just because of some decisions you made. Many times, you've allowed someone in your life to make your decisions for you. Sure, for some, this can be good. But for most of us, our life's decisions are best left up to us to make. If you've been allowing others to make your decisions, don't worry, you can always begin again.

First, ask yourself, "How do you want your world to function. How do you fill your life? What activities do you fill your time with? What goals do you create for yourself? What kind of people would you decide to share it with?" These choices are all yours to make. If you have decided to build your world successfully, you must have a Willingness to Win.

How big is your "Want to?" How strong is your desire to win? Are you sick and tired of the same circle? Have you backed yourself into a corner, or have you challenged yourself and said, "Enough is Enough! I want the things I desire, the things I deserve to have, and by any means necessary. I want to Win! I want to experience the peace that goes beyond understanding. I want to take care of myself better, as well as, the people I love. I want to live a healthier, more enjoyable life.

I want my finances to back me up instead of pulling me down. I want a defense when unforeseen things happen, or life throws an unexpected curveball. I want to be prepared to the best of my ability. I want to see ALL God's creations whether it's the blue water on an Island in the Caribbean or maybe the mountains of Colorado."

You have to OWN this, and get it in your spirit that this is your RIGHT, and you are entitled to it. As a friend of mine, Ms. Washington, might say "you want MORE."

This list of wants is vital. They touch the core of your soul, digging up those pains of not having what you desire, not being in your rightful place, or not being in your position in life. They are wants, that put your purpose into perspective. They force you to plan, prepare and execute. They give you an attitude of strength, a strong emotional desire, and they birth your willingness to win. *Damn, I just lifted my own spirit!!* YOU MUST KNOW THIS!!!

Energy is everything! No matter what, keep your energy up. Today's world of negative television, radio and, of course, the internet, plays an emotional roll in our lives. In short, we are surrounded by the negative.

I am not saying there aren't good and positive things to experience from these outlets; however, it's the negative information that infiltrates our emotions, dictating our energy to move downward into a non-effective state. This inundation of negativity, makes it challenging to draw positive energy to us, which is necessary in our process of progress.

When you have a willingness to win, you will start chipping away at any and everything that do not contribute to the advancement of you obtaining your goals in life. First thing on the list should be old bad habits. As I said before, the hardest challenge people have to come to grips with is that, "Change requires Change," and not partial change, but a full turn around.

If you're not happy about what you're doing at the moment, or where you currently are in life - pause. Stop and realize that whatever you have been doing up to this point, is what got you here, and now, it's time to create change.

I was watching an interview on YouTube featuring the rapper-turned-actor, Will Smith (who I consider a very hard working, motivated, and positive figure). He made a statement that was another, as Oprah would say, "light bulb moment." He said, "if you want to know who you are, look at the five people you are with the most, and if you don't like what you see, then change that."

So, what does that mean? Examine your surroundings. Part of your willingness to win has to include having the right people around you, in your circle, and with the right energy. I tell people all the time: a fighter is only as good as his corner.

Before you hear that bell, and jump into that ring, who are you listening to? Who is your trainer, your motivator, the person/people who pick you up when you fall, or make a mistake? Who looks out for your best interest, patches you up, and tells you what to watch out for?

There is an old saying that, "iron sharpens iron." Fill your circle of friends and associates with people who will support you, and cause you to be even sharper.

I'm sure that any successful person would tell you that, success and winning is not easy. Truthfully, it's not supposed to be. If it was, everyone would be successful. Not only will you have to embrace change, but depending on how you grew up, you may also have to embrace necessary struggle.

Yes, *necessary* struggle. It's like that resistance your muscles feel when stretching and pulling them at the gym. Sure it's a struggle in the beginning, but it is very necessary for your growth. It is that rose that pushes through the concrete, and then blooms. Oh how it struggled, but it was necessary!

Once, a little boy was playing outdoors and found a fascinating caterpillar. He carefully picked it up and took it home to show his mother. He asked his mother if he could keep it, and she said he could, if he took good care of it.

The little boy got a large jar from his mother, and put in plants for it to eat, and a stick to climb on. Every day, he watched the caterpillar and brought it fresh plants to eat.

One day, the caterpillar climbed up the stick and started acting strangely. The boy worriedly called to his mother, who came and understood that the caterpillar was creating a cocoon. The mother explained to the boy how the caterpillar was going to go through a metamorphosis and would transform into a butterfly.

The little boy was thrilled to hear about the changes his caterpillar would go through. He watched every day, religiously, waiting for the butterfly to emerge. One day, it happened: a small hole appeared in the cocoon and the butterfly started its struggle to come out.

At first, the boy was excited, but soon he became concerned. The butterfly was struggling so hard to get out! It looked like it couldn't break free! It looked desperate! It looked like it was making no progress!

The boy was so concerned he decided to help. He ran to get scissors and then walked back (because he had learned not to run with scissors). He snipped the cocoon to make the hole bigger and the butterfly quickly emerged!

As the butterfly came out, the boy was surprised. It had a swollen body and small, shriveled wings. He continued to watch the butterfly, expecting that, at any moment, the wings would dry out, enlarge, and expand to support the swollen body. He knew that in time, the body would shrink, and the butterfly's wings would expand.

But neither happened!

The butterfly spent the rest of its life crawling around with a swollen body and shriveled wings. It never was able to fly...

As the boy tried to figure out what had gone wrong, his mother took him to talk to a scientist from a local college. He learned that the butterfly was SUPPOSED to struggle. In fact, the butterfly's struggle to push its way through the tiny opening of the cocoon, pushes the fluid out of its body and into its wings. Without the struggle, the butterfly would never ever fly. Sadly, the boy's good intentions hurt the butterfly.

As you go through life, keep in mind that struggling is an important part of any growth experience. In fact, it is the struggle that causes you to develop your ability and strength to fly, and to soar to even higher heights.

Your willingness to win has to be a strong, relentless, determination to breathe and have the freedom you desire in life. Fight as if you were drowning in a pool, trying to swim to the top and suddenly, something wrapped around your ankle and grabbed you, trying to pull you back under.

At this point, giving up is not an option. If you want to live -you must fight. This is your willingness to Win!

How bad do you want it?

How strong is your desire to find and fulfill your purpose, and be who you are meant to be? Don't let fear win, don't let your past hold you hostage, and absolutely do not let people's negative influences deter you from your path. You are much bigger than you know, and more than worth it. Mind Set Go!

Chapter Seven

Let Love Getcha

I was in a restaurant one evening when I happened to look up, and there was a very tall and attractive young lady walking in. She had on a T-shirt that read "Do What You Love."

Now, you already know how I feel about believing in everything you see, hear, or have been taught; however, I am one that believes everything happens for a reason. I'm sure others in the restaurant saw the shirt as well. Nevertheless, it stuck out to me. After thinking to myself, "wow somebody gets it," I couldn't help but think there are a lot of people that don't.

There is so much more to life than a boss, a job that doesn't't give you fulfillment, or getting paid, just to pay bills. I always said, if I am working just to pay bills, then I probably, just won't have a job.

It amazes me to know that there are a lot of people out there, who have made life decisions, causing them to be stuck doing things they simply don't love. This can hinder everything around you. You start to feel stuck or trapped as if there is no way out. You find yourself going around in the same circle. You begin feeling unhappy about what you're doing, which causes you to operate on a lower vibration, in which, you can't draw the right opportunities to you.

Take control and make a decision to change and restore your energy to a higher vibration, which starts in your mind first.

You have to become motivated and know you are on your way out of what you're in. Start making plans and taking the authority to do what you love. You must Let Love get you! Now, of course, change doesn't happen overnight, especially when you have been doing the same thing for years. Yet, you have to start somewhere, or else, continue dealing with what you've *been* dealing with, and not being able to occupy the capacity you are called to fill.

Love is one of the strongest emotions we, as humans, have the privilege of possessing and experiencing. It breaks down barriers, pulls things together, lifts you up, and causes your drive to be even stronger.

Love gives your life a focus, as well as hope. It builds you up after being torn down, and most of all, it conquers all. Now, who wouldn't want to be a part of that kind of power, that kind of energy? It makes you think that Love is where it's at, and IT IS!

Love is doing what you enjoy, even if you're not getting paid.

Ask yourself right now: "what do you love to do and what would you do right now if money weren't a concern." Chances are, you have a talent, a gift, or simply just a passion for that something that constantly stays with you - it's like an itch that needs to be scratched. Trust me, it won't go away until you let love get you.

If I were to name all the people I am surrounded by that inspire me, taught me a few things, or gave me excellent advice, I'm pretty sure I would have to add at least ten more chapters to this book; however, there is one particular person that came to mind while writing this chapter.

My friend, Mr. Calvin "Nookie" Pruden, spent the early part of his life on the wrong side of the law. However, he has done a complete 180 and is now the devoted Muslim brother, Mr. Nadir Flowers. Two years ago, Mr. Flowers started an organization called "Humbled Helping Hands Initiative." They have an Awesome program that feeds the less fortunate and the homeless. One day, he reached out to me and told me how they were blessed to feed people for free, a few times a month, at different locations. They work for free and provide food off of donations they receive, and even out of their own pockets. I was more than impressed and asked how I could help out. He said while donations are great, it would be even better if I could come down to the center to see exactly what they do. I was so excited for him for stepping out and starting such a great, and much needed, program.

One Monday, I decided to head down to the center, but not alone. I called my team of five barbers up (including my oldest daughter). We walked in a hall-like setting with well decorated tables and chairs, already prepared with plates and utensils. In the back, Mr. Flowers was in the kitchen. He had his back turned to us as he was pouring hot spaghetti noodles into a strainer.

I came up behind him and said, "Man let me help with that!" He turned and smiled, "HEY!!!!!!" When he saw the whole crew, he really lit up. As he continued to pour the noodles in the strainer, he turned to me and said, "Man, thank you so much. Let's get ready because it's about to go down at noon."

Now, at the time, I already knew that people were coming to eat. What I didn't know was, it was going to be almost 150-200 people who would come walking through those doors. We only had an hour or so to get this done! Noon hit, and like clockwork, a long line had formed outside. People from all walks of life came through the doors, of all ages, even young children. We served everyone as if they were kings and queens. We wanted them to know that we were at their service, and here for *them*.

They were all kind, thankful, and appreciative. I didn't know everyone's personal situation, but I do know life can throw some mean curve balls, and we have no idea what caused them to be there that day. However, it didn't matter. What mattered, was the need that needed to be met.

This was truly an awesome experience. However the smile on Nadir's face impressed me the most. LOVE GOT HIM! He was so at peace and happy to do this for people, he had found his passion. His actions and love were overwhelmed with compassion, humility, and joy. Nadir looked at me and said, "now you see what we do." I responded, "Amazing." It wasn't about money. It wasn't about popularity or fame. This was a person that realized he was chosen for a purpose, and found it while being a blessing to so many others. Let LOVE GETCHA! Good Job Mr. Flowers.

MIND SET GO!!

For donations or more info for helping hands please visit: www.humbledhelpinghandsinitative.org

One thing for sure, you cannot be great without Enthusiasm, which in fact, is one of my favorite words. Enthusiasm is a Greek word that derived from the word "Theos" or "God," and "entheos," which means, Possessed by GOD, (I love this one) then later, in the early 17th century became enthusiasm, "God in you or inspired by God."

I absolutely love it! Doing what you love *requires* enthusiasm. Enthusiasm is contagious. The right people will gravitate toward you, wanting to contribute and be a part of what you're doing. You become possessed God, operating on a higher level, because of your freedom to do so.

I know plenty of people who hate Mondays after a weekend off. However, if the truth be told, MONDAY is not the problem; it's your job!

When you have chosen a job/career for every reason, *but love*, you didn't let love get you. You let bills get you, circumstances get you, influences of other people, and most times, a higher paycheck.

More money will definitely get you going, which is not bad, but it will not bring you the freedom, or satisfaction, or the fulfillment you desire. Freedom, satisfaction, and fulfillment come from your purpose in life, and this is where you generate that desire for change.

A while back, I attended an entrepreneurial seminar in Newark, Delaware. The speaker walked in, turned on his handheld microphone, and said, "When you have a job, you can't wait for retirement, but when you're doing what you love, you are already retired."

He had me from the door. I knew I had to let love get me. I knew I had to follow my desire and my passions. To me, it was the only way, and the window, to true freedom.

I must tell you this: you don't have to settle or put up with situations you don't deserve. You can succeed in having the life you desire. You can accomplish goals you never imagined you would complete. You just have to start.

Know your value. Know your worth. Capitalize off your gifts and talents. Use them to the max; explore new territories; take risk and chances; silence the fear in your mind; and do the work required for your goals - without ceasing.

Master your craft. Put the hours in by making the necessary sacrifices and bringing death to your old bad habits, and don't let the birth of the new you, be kidnapped again by the old you, once you're free.

I say to you: let LOVE get you and you will never be let down by disappointment again. Keep your energy up, have enthusiasm and be possessed by GOD. Let it lead you to your ultimate goal of PURPOSE, reminding you that you're bigger than you know, and once again MIND SET GO!

Faith requires work to execute results -
Work just needs to be Executed!

Chapter Eight

Brick By Brick

My father, the late Samuel Reed, L.I.P (Live in Peace) used to say, "Son you can't build a castle on quicksand." I have to laugh to myself, he was the type of man that knew that anything was possible.

My dad didn't have much school education, but in life, he had a PhD. All he knew was work work work. He'd say to me, "Take your time son, and do it right. GOD didn't make the earth in one day. Everything takes time, and remember you always have to build your way up and most of the time that takes brick by brick." My Dad was a construction worker. He did a lot of building in his career, as well as, paving sidewalks, home improvements, and bricklaying. His message to me was to always make sure my foundation was strong, he wanted to make sure that I understood that every brick counts, and is vital for my progress.

He used the example of the castle and the quicksand to represent the foundation, and with his many Life101 conversations, I couldn't help but learn a few life lessons. One of my favorite nuggets learned from him was, "The Shortcut is often timed the longest route" (see, I told you). After experiencing things in life, I still made some foolish choices by trying to take the shortcuts and end up paying for it big.

So what are some of the bricks I've placed in my foundation? Let's start with Effort.

Effort is a vigorously strong and determined attempt. Without effort, we simply would not move. Once we have made an internal commitment to ourselves to move forward towards achieving our goal, it is our effort that starts the ball rolling.

Notice I said internal commitment. I said that because I've realized early in life, we can say any and everything out of our mouth, but like I said before:

"You're not saying anything until you're doing something."

Talk is cheap and anyone can afford it. That's why, for a lot of people, all they have is talk with no effort. Time moves very quickly. Don't waste your TIME CURRENCY on just talking. Start being about it! Your goals, your dreams, and your visions are waiting to meet you.

I want you to get out of that old mindset of just talking about what you're *going* to do, or *want* to do, and start producing an effort to DO IT! In my opinion, one of the deadliest words in the English vocabulary is procrastination!

It will bring you to a moving standstill: time will keep moving on, while you're only thinking about moving forward. By standing still, you risk the chance of missing out on every opportunity that may come your way to help you elevate to the next level.

You must take the risk. Take the leap. So what if you fall flat on your face. So what if people look at you and laugh from the sidelines. YOU'RE PUTTING FORTH AN EFFORT, and that's much more than a lot of people can say.

Commitment is my next brick. You must be committed to what you want to do or achieve. Now, again, this is not something you just say you're going to do. It is an internal commitment made by the real you (the inner you) to hold yourself accountable, and to complete your journey towards your goal.

Trust me when I tell you, once you've added a commitment to your foundation, people and obstacles are going to come out the woodworks trying to distract you and deter you from your goals. Even lack of finances may come into play; however, you have to FIGHT and keep the MIND SET GO attitude.

All of these trials and tests that come, are just the universe's way of testing you to see if you really want to succeed, to see if you're serious about walking in your purpose, and to show you yourself. You have what it takes, and everything is all ready for you to succeed, you just have to commit and execute. Remember, the Universe is on your side, and not only that, the Universe needs you, just as much as you need it, to keep this masterpiece called life, alive and progressing.

My next brick is Focus. Now, before we get into this next brick, I'm sure you're probably wondering already, "how many bricks do you need or how many bricks are there?" Well, my question to you is: how big is the castle you're trying to build for yourself? The bigger your vision, the stronger your foundation must be to sustain, support, and uphold your vision.

I'm not a big gambler; however, I do make my way down to the casino every now and then. One particular casino I go to has live horse races. They have the most beautiful well-trained well-equipped horses I've ever seen, strong built legs of awesome muscle and power.

The trainers would walk the horses out to the track, with the jockeys already mounted on these majestic animals. I couldn't help but notice the blinders on the horses (actually, believe it or not the technical name is blinkers; however, we all know them as blinders). They are used to help the horse stay focused on track before him, and enable the horse to run his fastest race.

To become truly focused on your goals, you must put on your proverbial blinders, this is to limit any and all distractions that may hinder your progress. Now let me say this, it is not easy in the beginning. Over the years, we have created this world of ours that includes people's habits and routines that can, and will, be a distraction to you - IF you allow them to.

Your job is to recognize what's a distraction, and do what is necessary to block it out, using your blinders, so that your "Brick of FOCUS" can be executed.

How do you know if someone or something is a distraction? If it doesn't't contribute to, or fit into your goals, dreams, or vision you have set for yourself, then it is a distraction.

CONFIDENCE

Confidence is a simple, yet, vital brick you must have in your foundation. Having a lack of confidence will forfeit you from the game before you even begin. Your level of confidence is what will drive you, even when the rough road starts to persist.

Confidence can overpower fear, which is the number one cause behind why people fail to pursue their dreams and goals. Start today in building your confidence by setting small goals and achievements; making sure you successfully complete them, by sticking with it and not giving up.

Create a timeline, with some realistic, short-term goals, adding a definitive starting and ending point. After completing your goal, move onto the next. Things are not completed overnight. There can, and will be setbacks, which is fine, but pick up and keep going to the end. The more you accomplish, the more your confidence will grow. For instance...

About a year ago, I wanted to start working out and lose some pounds. I also wanted to build some muscle, as well as keeping my heart pumping for good health. So, I joined a gym. At the gym, I met a guy named Camara Keita (CK for short). CK was a fitness trainer and manager at the gym. He was known as "The Beast." Now, hearing this, and going to the gym for the first time in a *long time,* "The Beast" was intimidating. However, I wanted to change, and this was my guy. We met, and I told him my workout goals, which included being slimmer, cut up and ripped like a sports athlete. He laughed a bit but said, "It's definitely possible, if you are willing to go hard, put in the hard work and more importantly, change your diet."

I said, "Cool!"

On a Monday morning, as soon as I walked in the gym, CK yelled, "D. Reed you're here! Let's go meet over by the bench for chest and arms day."

I strolled over to the flat bench. All I saw was a weight bench with one weight bar on it, and no weights. CK comes over and says, "Okay, here is where we start. I need you to get under there and do about 15 to 20 reps, no weights."

Confused, I confirmed, "No weights?"

"Yes, no weights. This is what we will be doing for the next week or so. After that, I may add a few pounds on once I see you have the techniques down and are gaining strength."

See, when it came to lifting weights and working out, this was my first brick. The Bar was the beginning of me building a solid foundation of technique and skill. Again, as my Dad would say, "You can't build a castle on quicksand; foundation must be solid." The first brick is always a challenge, but, it may be the most important. I didn't have a problem with the bar. My problem, was my pride, and being concerned about other people seeing this grown man (ME) only lifting a 30-pound bar, and at times, struggling. CK knew what it would take for me to reach my goals. After a week went by, he started adding weights and then more weights, which was like adding more bricks. I was getting stronger, doing things I never thought I could do, and my technique was solid - I was finally growing. We started out with my first brick, which was the bar, and grew from there, brick by brick. I understand now why we started with the bar and I appreciate that.

Your first brick could be you starting a business, which requires a lot of groundwork in the form of promoting; going from door to door; delivering flyers; or posting up photos and information on social sites. Even when you're hearing negative feedback that may hurt your feelings, or be discouraging, I say, "so what?" Who cares what people think and how they feel? You are building from the ground up, with a goal in mind that you must accomplish. This doesn't't happen overnight or instantly. You must start at the bottom with one brick, developing technique and skills that will create for you a solid foundation, as you grow towards your goal.

Strong Corner
I'll add just one more brick to the foundation, which I think is major and that is... make sure you have a Strong Corner.

Remember the saying "A fighter is only as strong as his corner." The company you keep, the people around you the most, must be good assets to your goals and on the same vibration of success that you are.

Just as I said earlier, if you want to know who you are, check out the five people you engage with the most, and if you don't like what you see, then change that.

Who motivates you? Who is your Trainer? You may not know it yet, but we all look up to someone.

On this journey, it is always a good idea to have a mentor, or someone you respect that can be honest with you, and who has been down a few roads, good and bad, to give you proper guidance.

I hear people saying they want to change their life-style, rather is finance or poor eating habits, not realizing that the company they keep, may be bad influences. Listen let's keep in 100, the people you are around the most, close friends or family members, you simply can't just cut off. HOWEVER,...

In the process of change, you have to put a limit on your time spent with them. For instance, if you are trying to lose weight, you have to limit your time eating out with people who are constantly making trips to a Pizzeria. The same goes for a person who is driven and wants to succeed in life. It can be very difficult to be focused on your goals and driven, if your friend's idea of achieving goals is sitting in front of a television, playing the latest sports PlayStation or Xbox game. We must pay attention to the people in our circle and make sure if they're in our corner, they need to be contributing to our success, in one way, or another.

I honestly could go all day laying bricks for a foundation; however, this is your foundation. You know what's important to you, as well as your strong points and weaknesses. The key things are making sure the bricks you lay are strong, solid, and in place. Once you start to build your foundation, stick to it, depend on it, lean and rely on it. Stay Focused, be confident, and endure to the end. (As we move forward to the later chapters, I will thoroughly break down your CIRCLE and your CORNER people, and trust me, I can't wait. It's going to be life-changing.)

MIND SET GO!!!!! Remember In this process you can never allow yourself to forget that you are building and on this journey, you must build brick by brick.

Chapter Nine

Relationship Goals

So, like most of us in the new tech-savvy world, I'm big on social media. However,

I think it's incredible to be out in public and see so many of us simultaneously burying our heads into a small lit screen, while out to dinner, with an actual person sitting across from us. How did we get here? Nevertheless, I must admit there are some awesome things that come along with social media as well.

Every now and then a meme is posted, a video goes viral, or some sort of theme or phrase becomes the new hit. Well, I was on Facebook one day, and I noticed a pattern of people posting videos of couples doing wonderful and positive things with each other. Each video or pic was hash tagged #RelationshipGoals. Ah ha! The lights came on again.

Let me say this: being a business-minded individual is a catch 22. The good thing is that I'm always thinking of business ideas, the bad thing is, everything isn't about business. Although in this particular situation, the words "Relationship Goals" were about business to me.

Another important element you must have, that requires a lot of work, is building relationships. I tell people all the time that it's about who you know, and more importantly, who knows you. It doesn't't matter what job or career you're in or going for; if you're starting your own business; or simply just pursuing your dreams and goals, your job is to build healthy relationships, with positive people, wherever you go.

The fact of the matter is, no one really makes it on their own. There is always a need for someone with an insight or an expertise that you may not have, that can be a great contribution to you. Again, this requires you set your mind on being open for opportunities and building healthy, positive, relationships.

I'm sure by now, you can feel my emphasis on *healthy, positive,* relationships. Naturally, all relationships don't end up that way, which is okay. Still, please make a note-to-self, "you cannot afford to have any toxic relationships, especially when it comes to business."

As you're building your business, your career, or your brand, be mindful of your relationships. This is not say you're going to always be perfect, or say and do the right things, but people are always watching and listening; they have absolutely no problem with yelling out your failures and mistakes but will *whisper* your accomplishments and successes.

I was watching a reality series a few years ago called, *Run's House*. It was based on the home life of hip-hop, icon rapper, Rev. Run, from the legendary hip-hop group Run-DMC. In this particular episode, Run's oldest son, Joe Joe, was trying to branch out on his own into the music industry. The two of them decided to go to lunch, and have a focused discussion on Joe Joe's career, and how to become a successful artist. Joe Joe was looking to his dad to gain some insight and tips on where to start, and the do's and don'ts of the business.

Now, surprisingly, when they sat down to talk, Run asked Joe, "Have you tried talking to your Uncle Russ?" Joe Joe replied, "Not yet."

"Well," Run said, "You should talk to him as soon as you have the chance." Uncle Russ is Mr. Russell Simmons, the music mogul that started Def Jam Records, kicking off successful careers such as RUN-DMC, Kurtis Blow, L.L Cool J, and countless more.

He is also a media and fashion mogul, and arguably, one of the most influential, successful, African American Men in America today.

Now Run continued to talk with his son and told him, "You need to talk to your Uncle Russ because he is GIFTED! He has a gift for bringing people together!!" Ah ha!!! The lights came on once again for me. RELATIONSHIPS.

It today's world, it seems that everything is geared towards negativity and separation.

Social sites can be cruel at times, generating a lot of energy focused on keeping us all in constant competitions, battles, and wars. Often times, it's with people we don't even know. I have come to realize that bad, and even toxic, relationships can be a major setback or downfall if you allow them to persist.

As a focused person that has a purpose, you have zero time for unhealthy relationships. Your goal is to Build Build Build, whether it's with family members that are like-minded, close friends, or someone you have met that carries the right attitude, focus, and goals.

I am always looking for people that I can connect with, that are where I would like to be in life or possess the things I want to have in life.

I want to talk with them, learn what I can from the path they took, and the ups and downs behind how they achieved their goals. Almost everyone that comes along on your path could be a potential door, or vehicle, to advance you to the next level.

I think that building relationships with the right people is a must. Starting today, realize that you cannot afford to be negative, which can be a turnoff for a lot of potential successful people. You need as much help, guidance, and gifts from the outside as you possibly can receive.

Be mindful that as you're building relationships, you may also be Brand Building (which I will discuss in more detail in a later chapter). Also, be mindful of your social surroundings. Your social surroundings are whatever you put out there for people to see and know about the person you are. Think about the way you want people to view you; think about how you want to be treated and respected. Your social media, for example, is an extension of you; so whatever you decide to put out there, whether it's negative or positive, is how people watching will perceive you, and trust me, *they are watching*.

As I said before, we are building, and we need as many bricks as possible. Building great relationships with great people is always a great idea. So again, once your mind is Set it's time to Go. You Got It: Mind Set GO!! You can do it. You are *way* bigger than you know. You just have to KNOW IT!

Now, let's go a little deeper on relationships as I introduce to you another side of relationship goals. These are what I call, "The relationship goal barriers," which, may prevent you from even pursuing business relationships from the start.

Yes, there are some barriers that will keep you from getting yourself out there and known. The first is....

Fear
This may be the singlehanded, most dangerous, Relationship Goal Barrier on the list and had to be listed as #1. Fear will not only stop you dead in your tracks, but it will prevent you from even starting your journey. This word has to be dealt with immediately! Fear of failing; fear of what others may think of you; fear of stepping out of your

comfort zone; fear of becoming who you are or meant to be in this life. Fear is like a disease, and when you have it, you must get rid of it asap by using the only known cure, and doing as Nike says, "Just Do It!"

Anti-social

If you consider yourself an anti-social person, then building relationships with others is not only a challenge, it's damn near impossible. If you find that you are not interested in starting conversations with people, or going to networking events or other social gatherings, this could be one of the reasons holding you back from Success.

I'm sure we've all heard the saying, "The squeaky wheel gets the oil." And it's true. Maybe you have a product you want people to start using, or a business you would like to start. Well, guess what? People won't know anything about you, or your product, if you are not willing to take a step. Take the necessary risk to get out there and MAKE SOME NOISE!

If you take an orange and squeeze it, what happens? Orange Juice comes out of course, and that's because Orange Juice was in it already. We as human beings are way more than meets the eye.

You are so much bigger than you know. One of our problems is that we do not embrace the moments we are being squeezed by a situation, a dilemma, or maybe even a person testing us. Instead, often times, we act out. The correct response would be for us be to settle down, relax, and begin observing what is going on inside us. We need to start controlling our emotions by first acknowledging the power and the energy behind what we are experiencing. Second, it should be corrected if it's negative, this way, in the future, we aren't expressing that same negativity. Third, you need to channel that power and that energy into something positive that will work in your favor.

Homebody

Unless you have a home-based business that is success-ful, giving you a peace of mind and making money, you are going to have to get yourself out there. Yes, leave your home aka your comfort zone.

This is very crucial. Our reliance on television and social media makes it easy to become a homebody. A homebody is truly a relationship goal barrier.

I'm not saying you have to attend every social event or community town hall meeting. What I *am* saying is, there are times you need to get out in the public-- especially if your career or business requires clientele. People want to see you and what you're about. Like a campaign, you become the first representative of your product or company.

Lack of Confidence

If I can be honest, one of the main reasons for writing this book was because, in my profession, I get to experience people from all walks of life. One of the things that sticks out to me about people is, there are so many of us that carry a lack of confidence - which is actually rooted in fear.

Some of are afraid to just simply try, or even take a chance. I mentioned in earlier chapters how the biggest risk in life, in my opinion, is not taking a risk. On the other hand, the most successful people thrive on taking risks.

You may find this hard to believe or understand, but there are a lot of people out there who are also afraid of Success. They are afraid of the attention it may bring or even the lifestyle change. Success also carries a sense of responsibility, which also may be a hurdle for some people to jump over.

Being a good leader requires confidence. When you try to build relationships with others, they want to see your confidence. They want to know that you believe in yourself and your product.

Never Doubt that you can exceed even further by pushing yourself beyond your comfort zone. I truly understand that the lack of confidence could result from trying and failing. This is when you've tried to do everything to Make It Happen, and things still didn't go your way - definitely not a good feeling. Yet, you still have to keep pushing.

Yes, I know how hard that is, but if anything is worth having in life, it's worth fighting for.

Being afraid to fail is being afraid to EXCEL. You must keep going; you're on the road to realizing you are bigger than you know, can do much more than you think, and go much further than you have ever gone before in life. Now set your mind and GO!

When I started to put together my list of Relationship Goal Barriers, I have to be honest, I hesitated to list this next barrier because it may stir up some things or may be a touchy subject for some. Well here goes nothing. My next Relationship Goal barrier is…

The Wrong Companion

Let's be real, we all want someone by our side, that's there in support of our goals and dreams. We want that one person who understands our lifestyle, as well as, our drive and ambition to achieve our goals in life.

It's always a plus to have a good support system with you on your life journey. However, when that significant other becomes a barrier, preventing you from building a business relationship with others due to insecurities, jealousy or even viewing you as competition towards them, it may become a problem.

Everyone has some sort of talent or gift that is connected to our Passion. These gifts and talents are spiritually given to us, by our Creator, to stir up, to use, and share with the world. They are needed for a specific task or job that helps keep our world functioning. Now, if that sounds huge and important, that's because it is…

So important that you cannot afford to forfeit it by having the wrong companion. A companion that has you emotionally shackled, with your aspirations and goals on lockdown, will prevent you from achieving your goals. The necessary relationships you must build, will connect you to the dots, all the way to the finish line.

Fortunately, most of the time our companions see things in us we don't see (i.e. they may already know that you're bigger than even you know).

They already know you can run a company; they are already aware that you can be the CEO, travel the globe, and become even larger than life. They have a clear understanding about your life, your gift, and motivation, because they themselves have the same passion and desires; and are conscious in knowing the importance of relationship building, knowing yourself, and executing your mission in life.

Now that you understand the importance of Relationship Goals and putting yourself in position to build them, it's time to act on it. Mind Set Go! Recognize opportunity when it comes; it could be in the form of a conversation at the carwash, at the food market or a networking event. Start preparing yourself for the transition to greatness and allowing success to happen. Let the noise of your greatness be heard. Let your gifts and talents be shared and used, so you may be advanced even more. Keep talking, keep advancing, and most of all KEEP BUILDING your relationship goals.

Circle people are good; Corner People are a must.

If you haven't noticed by now I love sports! I mean who doesn't't in this day and age? For me, it's more than just a game. I like to sift out the messages involved that pertain to our everyday life. As I just mentioned, there are two kinds of people in your life: circle people and corner people. When we think about the sport of boxing we think of fighters (boxers), the ring, corners, and ropes. I'm also sure most of us also think of Champions, lights, cameras, action, and money.

In 2017, Floyd Mayweather defended his title against Conor McGregor, going for his 50th win. Now, whether you like Floyd Mayweather or not, that's is up to you; however, we must agree his career as a boxer is outstanding and his record is incredible, especially now that he won and gained that 50-0 plus 300 Million! WOW!

Now, what does that have to do with your circles and corners? Well, I'm glad you asked. I went back and watched a few old fights. Actually not the fights, but the introductions of each fighter. I wasn't surprised to find that each fighter had the same kind of introduction: they all came in with music playing, lights flashing, and a group of people along side of the fighter or in the background, holding up championship belts, and cheering him on as they came through the crowd. These are...

The Circle People
They are the ones the fighter picked to surround him as he enters the arena. Some are there to symbolize that they know the Champ and/or connected to him. Some are there for the show - the glitz and glamour of the event. Some are there to get noticed or to promote themselves

for whatever agenda they have going on personally. Some are there to make sure if anything goes down (good or bad) they can say they were there for the fighter.

There are also a few people there simply because the person in the front is the current Champ, and as soon as they lose, these people will leave this Champ and move on to the next Champ.

When building relationships, it is so important to get a clear understanding of what type of people you're cool with occupying your circle (the people around you). We all have our own circles, our crew, squads or what have you, that we like to have around us for whatever reasons. However, at a certain point, you'll look around and wonder, "Where did my circle people go?" As a leader, this is, often times, a hard pill to swallow considering most of the time, you are always there for them.

It's like everyone benefits off you, and when things go south, they are no longer there for you. It's funny because I hear a lot of people, including myself, at one time bragging about their circle. Trust me, I'm definitely not saying you shouldn't't have one. By all means, your circle is needed for a purpose. What I am saying is know who they are, and why they are in your circle. So who are the important people around you?

The Corner People
As the Fighter continues to make his way down the aisle, getting closer to the ring, he walks up the steps solo, goes

through the ropes, and enters the ring. All of the circle people become irrelevant and the only people that matter right now is the fighter and his corner.

-YOU choose your circle, Corner people must *agree* to be in your corner.

There is a major difference between the people in your circle and the people that are in your corner. As part of your relationship goals, it is VITAL to have good "corner people." As the fighter goes to the corner between each round, there are usually two or maybe three people in his corner at the most; however, there's a guarantee to be two: the trainer and the cutman.

These people could care less about the music, the lights, camera, action, or the people yelling and screaming for you. They don't care about your feelings or what you have or don't have. They are not there to outshine you or have any hidden agendas to propel themselves above you. They have only one goal, and one concern, that is to see you WIN AND BECOME VICTORIOUS! YOU NEED YOUR CORNER PEOPLE!!!!!

My GOD, there is a difference!! I had to learn this. In this ring called LIFE, you must have a motivated trainer in your corner. When the rounds of life get rough, and you get out there and makes some wrong decisions, bad choices, and get knocked down a few times, you're going to need a trainer. They will remind you who you are, how you made it this far, and of the gifts and talent you possess that will make it possible for you to get back up and WIN!

And then there is the cutman.......

The cutman bandages you up covering up your wounds, so the opponent won't see your flaws. He stops the bleeding so you won't look vulnerable, like an easy target. The cutman helps take the swelling down, cools you off, doesn't't say much, but through his job - speaks volumes. There may be some circle people you can't share everything with. You can't let them know your weaknesses or flaws because they talk too much, and can't wait to tell everybody, so you can be exposed. That's why there should only be a few people that can make it to your corner.

You see, unlike some circle people, the trainer and the cutman are all about you. They are not loud; they deal strictly with you one-on-one, eye-to-eye, to help refocus you. They cover you, "yeah I see you made a few mistakes out there that caused you to get hit, but here, put this Band-Aid on, let me wrap this up, so no one will know."

#Relationshipgoals find you some good corner people. It's well worth the search.

Circle people are good to have, but your corner people are a must. MIND SET GO!

Chapter Ten

Free The Hostage

If there is any chapter in this book that I view as very important, vital, and emotional for me it has to be this one right here.

The word Hostage feels violent. It's very dark for me, whether it is physical, mental, or even spiritual. Anyone in this type of bondage is undoubtedly in an uncomfortable situation. Hostage means: a person seized or held as security for the fulfillment of a condition. Synonyms for Hostage are captive, prisoner, inmate, detainee, or even pawn.

One Saturday evening, I was invited to a women's group at a community center. The only male figure there, hopefully, with ALL the right answers women wanted to know about MEN!! *Yeah right*. I laughed at first, but then, I thought, "Wow, why not?" In fact, the idea became more interesting to me the more I thought about it.

So I agreed to show up at the community center. The group started at 7pm. When I arrived the ladies led me to my seat. The conversation was already underway. The topic for the group of ladies was "Women's Empowerment -Living Beyond our Beauty," hosted by a courageous young lady.

The discussion was mainly about them finding their strength again, conquering the pain of their past and bringing something more to the table other than outer beauty. It was an awesome idea turned into action, and I was honored to be a part.

The women were instructed to anonymously jot down a question or concern. Depending on what type of question it was, they wrote whether it was written to gain a male point of view or female point of view. Although, some questions were simply for the whole group's input or discussion.

Now, of course, everything was confidential and what was said there stayed there. In fact, I didn't even ask any of the women their names, but just from observing the circle I would say the ages ranged from 18-40.

They were all sincere, and I could tell by the vibe that some of them had deep hurts. A few of them had been through personal ordeals they hadn't mentioned to anyone. As I sat there and answered a few questions, in hopes of helping some of the ladies, I felt growth in myself.

My compassion and respect elevated even more for women, as I was enlightened by the stories of what some women have dealt with, and for some, still go through.

Some of the personal stories squeezed my heart a few times. I even felt myself trying to be strong for them and expressing empathy. There were instances such as physical abuse, verbal abuse and even some deeper things you could imagine. It was pretty intense and deep, some experienced abuse from strangers, but some suffered at the hands of close relatives.

There was one young lady who had a question on how to deal with something concerning a child. For a minute there, when questions came my way, I was ready, responding without hesitation. However, this was a question directed towards the group, and personally, my initial thought was, "I don't want any parts," due to its sensitive nature. I let the question bounce around for a few. If I can be honest, I truly felt at the time, I didn't even have an answer.

Then all of a sudden it got quiet. Now, the week before this event, I was writing a chapter in this book. I looked up at her and said, "FREE THE HOSTAGE." She zeroed in on me as if I found the key to the lock she desperately needed open. I said to her again, "You must Free the Hostage. The person that is in prison is you, and the person that is holding you hostage is YOU!"

I think so many times, we feel guilty for things that were done to us. We feel like we should have been on guard. We should have picked up on the signs; we shouldn't't have trusted that person that ultimately let us down in the first place. That is not a good feeling or easy to get over. We then feel that squeeze on us, and what may come out could be bitterness or resentment, which is not good, *but not all bad either.* In fact, if we allow ourselves to become more present and more conscious, this could be an opportunity to face these emotions and conquer them, releasing you to move towards your freedom.

Why did I mention this? Why did I take this route? Well... I want you to understand how important you are, how valuable you are, and the fact that there are gifts, talents, and a calling that you must use for your benefit and others. These are the things that will elevate you and make room for you to prosper and become successful. It can become very challenging to achieve your goals or purpose in life IF you are NOT free. It is a must that you FREE THE HOSTAGE, once your mind is set, it's time to GO!

I was overwhelmed by the fact that so many women had stories or situations they been through in the past, or going through currently, and were still dealing with the pain. I had to write this chapter on Freeing the Hostage because, whether we know it or not, a lot of us won't allow ourselves to move forward, because we are holding ourselves hostage to our past.

A part of us feels, "Why try? I'm just going to fail anyway. Why care? No one ever cared for me. What's wrong with me? Why didn't they want me? What did I do? I didn't do anything wrong to deserve to be treated this way." Guess what? You are correct. Just as a person in jail wishes to be physically free, I think it's just as important, if not more important, to be mentally free.

Being mentally and spiritually free is a requirement for success. If your idea of success is just a nice car, a house, or even a college degree, then fine, keep working hard and you will have your success. Keep in mind while these things are GREAT to have - they are temporary. The success I'm talking about is the freedom of finding you. Being the best YOU that you can possibly be and by finding your true happiness, which is found in your purpose. The problem is we continue get in our own way by holding ourselves captive to the past, which keeps us stagnant in the present, and unable to control and create our future.

When I was about twenty-six years old, I bought my first home. It was a 4 bedroom townhouse with a big back-yard. The backyard walked out to a brick patio, which was cool, but I always wanted a nice huge deck. My dad was getting older; however, he was the kind of man that never says "NEVER."

I asked him to help me build the deck and, of course, he was all in. We gathered all the materials and began to build. The whole project took about one week to finish. When it was all completed... WOW! I must say that the deck was well put together, and huge.

A few weeks later, one morning I walked out onto my deck, in my PJs, with some flops on and I felt something snag and then catch the bottom of my pants leg. I moved to the side, knelt down, and saw that a few of the nails weren't nailed all the way into the wood. I called my dad and told him that we may have to thoroughly look over the whole deck to make sure everything was nailed down.

He said, "Well, let's get right to it, right now." It may seem like something minor but it could've been a major is-sue if someone walked out there tripped, fell and got hurt. Now normally when someone uses the phrase "nailed it," "nail it down," etc. it's usually doing something great, but this was a little different for me. The nail pops that was coming up from the boards on the deck were a problem, a bit dangerous and could cause harm if not taking care of. I looked at them as unresolved issues which needed immediate attention.

We all have dealt with unresolved issues in our lives, at some point. I call them the silent killers that can snag and cause you to keep tripping over and over again, in the same spot. Eventually someone could get hurt and the reason is the same: everything hasn't truly been nailed down.

The moment you make up your mind and its set on go mode to free yourself, you must immediately deal with the unresolved issues.

You have to make sure all your issues are nailed down. Every now and then it is very important to give ourselves a quick self-examination: a mental and spiritual walkthrough if you will. Your nail pops in life could be an issue from childhood, or potentially relationship problems, I say, Nail it down. There may be regrets you have, that old shoul-da, coulda, woulda, if only I… Nail it down. These are all things that, in our minds, we think we need to hold on to, but the reality is these things are holding onto you. The power is always in your possession to "Free the Hostage."

Let now be the time that you finally take the keys of knowledge, power, and control to, once and for all, free yourself. Free yourself from pains, mistakes, situations, and people that you have allowed to take over your mind, holding yourself hostage to, and ultimately rendering you unable to move. Let's start nailing down every issue that keeps popping up in our lives so we won't allow them to snag us again.

FREE THE HOSTAGE simply because, enough is enough, and you deserve better. You deserve to live your life to the fullest, and walk in what God has called you to be, for your purpose. MIND SET GO!!!

Why just be free and exist when you can be free and LIVE!

Chapter Eleven

Game On

Two days before this chapter, I lost not only a good friend, but a little brother, to cancer. I can feel that a great part of me is hesitant to write anything, let alone a whole new chapter. My soul is grieving because of the loss, and somehow, a part of me is focused on answers, reasons, and what lesson is to be learned from this. One of the many things I do know is that life is precious, and time waits for no one. I find myself telling hard working people all the time, "In all that you're getting in life never forget about LIVING your life," L.I.P Akeem Lee.

In all that I am sharing with you in the book, please do not miss the main point. I am expressing the importance of LIVING YOUR LIFE and succeeding on your own terms.

Life can, and will throw curveballs every now and then, and sad to say, some of them can be devastating; and unfortunately, there's just no way to ever be fully prepared. Each morning you wake up is another chance to begin...again!

The moment you walk out your front door there should be a reminder going off inside of you saying: "GAME ON."

A good friend of mine named, Neil Carr, is a successful rising-star actor, he always says, "Be ready, so you won't have to get ready!"

A Game On attitude should ignite a fire inside you. It is like the HVAC guy (heating and air conditioning) coming over to relight the pilot on your heater. First, there is a strong whoosh sound from the pilot being lit, then the heat starts moving through the air vents. Suddenly, things start to warm up all around you, as you realize the power is on and being circulated. That's exactly how you should feel when a great idea enters into your mind. You've just been LIT!

Once it has been LIT, you cannot allow your flame to be put out by anyone. It is your responsibility to make sure you prevent anything from hindering your purpose or accomplishing your Goals, nor can you allow anyone to stop you or take you off course. Remember to STAY LIT!

Allow me to ask you this: Are you a good person? Do you care about other people's well-being and success? Are you the good friend that wants the best for everyone, even if it means settling for the back seat, the short end of the stick, keeping quiet, or letting everyone go before you?

Let me first applaud you for a job well done! You are one Awesome person! HOWEVER........

There is a time you MUST put yourself FIRST (pause and think). There is a time where you CAN NOT pour into everyone else's cup, especially when yours is nowhere near full. I'm sure all the above sounds wonderful, and Jesus, Buddha, and Muhammad are smiling down upon you. BUT there are times you need to come with a FEE!!! This is a GAME ON attitude mode.

I already know what you are thinking, "I need to get paid for what I do?" Yes! That may be true. BUT the F.E.E. I am talking about is a must have at varying points of your life. Listen carefully, and I don't mean to offend anyone reading this book, but while you're on this journey to success and personal fulfillment you must come with a FEE and that is......

*F**K EVERYBODY ELSE (FEE)*

You heard me loud and clear! Listen, do not be fooled. People love you. Yes, they do, but not as much as they love themselves. People do care about you, but not as much as they care about themselves. People will be excited about you going after your dreams and goals, but definitely not as excited as they are about their own dreams and goals. The word selfish gets a bad rap but the truth is Sometimes you have to be selfish. Sometimes you have to go for yours when it comes to winning and achievements - it's GAME ON, and this is definitely A MIND SET GO STATE!!

The fact of the matter is, at the end of the day, we all came here naked and solo, and trust me that's how we're all leaving. With that being said, GAME ON mode is an attitude that will also allow you to enter into a now or never mindset. Please, let me be clear about being selfish, I am truly NOT saying for you to not have consideration for others and their life situations-- especially the people who are close to you. I AM saying there is a time, even as a goodhearted person, when you must put yourself first, and focus on YOU!

There are people in your life that need you to cross that finish line. They need you to open some windows, some pathways, that they can follow through. This is merely the reason why we need people around us that understand the movements of our goals of success, and how to get there.

They understand that we are all trying to make it happen in our lives. If someone shows the signs of being a true, fighting, champion - they are in GAME ON MODE. We all need to rally behind them to push them through, with hopes that once they get in, they will unlock the doors for all of us. However, if you do not have these type of people around you, with that type of MINDSET, then it's time for you to display your FEE attitude and become the warrior you are, and go after what is rightfully yours.

I have come to realize that everything starts with your MINDSET and that's why I came up with the phrase, "MIND SET GO". Even though you think it, or even believe it, you have to act on it and move forward.

Champions operate different from everyone else, while you're sleeping they are up. When people say "NO," they say "YES." When we yell out "'CAN'T," they say "CAN." Some people say, "Well this is the way we've been doing it." Champions say, "This is the new way we're doing this NOW!" It's GAME ON. Do you want it or not? Are you tired of being where you are? GOOD!

Rob Siltanen wrote, "Here's to the crazy ones. The misfits. The rebels. The troublemakers. The round pegs in the square holes. The ones who see things differently. They're not fond of rules. And they have no respect for the status quo. You can quote them, disagree with them, glorify or vilify them. About the only thing you can't do is ignore them. Because they change things.

They push the human race forward and while some may see them as the crazy ones, we see genius. Because the people who are crazy enough to think they can change the world, are the ones who do."

Here's to changing your piece of the world by taking new steps forward, which, in turn, changes someone else's world, which in turn, changes another's world... and another's...

Game on is an attitude. It's the focus of a lion on the hunt; the awakening of the warrior that lives inside you; the drive in you. That resilience that persistently keeps you getting back up again and again. That feeling of "I'm ready muthafuckas! Give me what's mine or I'm taking it because it belongs to me, and it's my right!"

Now, listen you don't have to say any of this out loud. Again, this is the "ATTITUDE" you should have when you're in GAME ON mode.

MIND SET GO!!!

There is a story I was told some years ago, and the sad thing is I can't even remember where I got it from, or who shared it with me. In any event, it was profound and it stuck with me. Therefore, I make it my business to share it with as many people I can to inspire them always keep their minds in a MIND SET GO state.

There was a General who had an army. He and his men set out to sea for a battle in a distant island. The journey was long, and many nights they had terrible storms that rocked their ship back and forth through the night. They arrived at their destination, and docked on the foreign island. All the men got off the ship and started walking on the island, getting themselves, and their equipment ready for battle. Suddenly, the General lit a few torches on the beach and begin to throw the lit torches into the ship, which they arrived in. The ship started to catch fire and burn in the water.

All of the soldiers were horrified and couldn't understand why the General would do such a thing. So, they asked him, "Why would you burn down our only means of transport to return back from where we came?"

The General smiled and told all of his men, "LISTEN TO ME. We have arrived here for one reason, and one reason only, that is to conquer. Either we will be warriors and win here, taking over the land, or we'll die here giving it all we got. We are not going back from whence we came. That's why I burned the ship. We are here to WIN, CONQUER, and take over this land." You need to be like the General. It's GAME ON, MIND SET GO MODE!! Never forget you are here to WIN, and once you leave your place of comfort "BURN THAT SHIP," because we are not going back.

It's funny, I have a good friend, Mr. Greg Lloyd, who is an awesome playwright and film director. You name it; he can do it. He and I always seem to show up at the same places or events. I actually told him this story a few years back, and every time he sees me, he points at me and says, "Burn that ship," and I always reply "I ain't going back." Then he would say, "Hey D, the extra mile is never crowded!" I would smile and say, "Yes very few go that way. GAME ON!"

Wake up and live like you've never lived before and look forward to an even greater tomorrow.

Chapter Twelve

Bigger Than You

Here we are, the final chapter. It's funny when I first decided to write this book, this chapter was the first thing that came to mind. All of the other chapters then followed. This particular chapter carried so much power and energy, that it felt like I needed to really prepare myself to write it. So, I began to write the other chapters first. Finding time to meditate and listen in silence for authentic and organic answers, I wanted to know which angle or way to deliver it, without sounding religious. I wanted to make sure this chapter tied up this whole book, and gave you a clear understanding of its message.

I've always been the type of person that analyzes situations and wants a deeper understanding of the world around me. *I guess that's the zodiac sign Cancer in me.* I remember thinking as a child about making a difference in the world for the better and making a great impact in others' lives. But why? Why care? Why do some of us take heed to the call of going beyond ourselves to do for others?

What is that internal pull that seems to whisper in your spirit, "You should do more. You are greater than you know; you have the ability to make a difference in this world." Even as you become an adult, you will notice the call getting stronger. That whisper grows until it begins to feel like a sense of urgency. And if that pull, or that call, doesn't't get a response soon, you'll begin to feel incomplete, as if you have unfinished business to handle.

I will never sit here and pretend I have all the answers. What I do know is that we didn't get the opportunity to choose our gifts, our talents or our purpose. Surprise! Funny, all this time you thought you had something to do with it. Wrong and Nope! LeBron James, Michael Jackson, Michael Jordan, all had nothing to do with choosing their talents. Matter of fact, in some way it seems these talents chose them - given to them without a choice.

I'm sure you've heard the saying, "Nothing in life is free." Well, I wouldn't say nothing. But I will say, most things worth having will cost you something, whether it's money, knowledge, or your time. There is a reason I spoke throughout this book on the importance of your time, gifts, talent, and purpose. These things are all connected, and were given to you to be utilized.

This thing we call life is a fully functional system in which, we are all a part of, and not by chance. Everything and everyone has a purpose, a job, a duty, and a mission to accomplish to keep this amazing system running smoothly. We are all connected, every one of us, whether we agree or not. Our purposes are not the same, but all are important.

I honestly feel that we owe a sense of gratitude for being here on this planet. Using our gifts and talents is much bigger than we can imagine, and with a purpose that is much bigger than we are.

They say to learn about life, you must pay attention to its creations. You must recognize the beauty in their workmanship by paying close attention to the detail in their craft. Before catching the writer's bug, my craft and career was as a professional barber/instructor. I started cutting hair at the age of 13.

A good friend of mine named, Robert Boulden, found a pair of haircutting clippers in his house that belonged to his mother. Now, these weren't just any pair of cutting clippers; they were professional clippers by one of the best companies that made hair clippers. They were ANDIS, and why they were at Robby's house, I have no idea...but they were his mother's.

Robby said, "Man, we should start cutting hair." I was like, "Okay." We wanted to start with the kids around the neighborhood. We both lived in the projects, and, as I said before, there were a lot of kids in the projects during that time, in the early 80's, that really couldn't afford haircuts. Rob would cut the kid's hair, and he would let me edge the cuts up at the end.

I remember sitting there in my bedroom, which was only but so big. We would set a stool up between the beds and start the cutting. I was anxiously awaiting my turn with the clippers. I know what you're thinking, "Wow, these two young men were cutting these young kids hair and sending them on their way." NOPE! We were practicing and butchering these kids' haircuts: uneven parts/lines in their heads, as wide as a four-lane highway in Atlanta. Some wanted boxed haircuts or to have their afros trimmed - but left my mom's house bald headed.

Robby continued to cut hair for a few years and then decided to do something different. However, I continued to cut hair and took my craft even further. After working in a real barbershop for a few years, I decided to get a professional license. Then, I opened up a few barbershops of my own. I became very popular for my signature haircuts. I would arrive at my shop at 7 am to long lines waiting out the door.

Most of my clients would start lining up at 4 am. YES, 4 am!! I would arrive, and it would be a festival of car doors, opening and shutting, of people rushing in line, arguing about who was there first. It was A MADHOUSE!! I eventually went to doing appointments only, which made things much easier.

In the beginning of this chapter, I mentioned that you can learn a lot about a creator by the creation. You can also learn about an artist through their body of work: the way it's detailed, the way it's laid out, or the type of messages it conveys on the canvas.

A professional barber, I was known for the detail in my cuts, the cleanness, and the symmetry of my lines. There is quite a bit you can learn about me just from my cut creations. I am a very detailed person; I love things to be in order and on point. I consider myself very professional, and care a great deal about my client's appearance and their satisfaction.

I decided to take my career to the next level of being an instructor, which landed me at the head of the table on The Board of Cosmetology and Barbering of the State of Delaware as the President.

Being a barber changed my life for the better. I must say, I love seeing so many walks of life, meeting so many great people, and watching their families grow generation after generation. I've seen people at their highest points, on down to their lowest; I've witnessed people get married starting a new life; and I've seen couples go through hard times that ended in divorce. I've seen people become new fathers and mothers, and I've also witnessed some losing a child.

There were even times, I became a family member of someone that didn't have a family. The craft of barbering introduced me to something much bigger than cutting hair, which was just one of my gifts and talents. It was not always about business, or about me. It taught me how I was much bigger than myself. I became a father to the fatherless, a big uncle to some and, most of the time, an ear to listen to when needed. I embraced this as I've gotten older— seeing the bigger picture of my purpose to inspire people, and to be that light of encouragement for everyone that comes in contact with me.

I realized my purpose was bigger than me, just as your purpose is also bigger than you.

No one is useless

Everyone has a purpose given to them. Everyone has a job to do that's bigger than them. We all are bigger than we know. Take a look around you, notice the detail in the sky, the trees, the mountains, and the ocean, all displaying their own uniqueness. The colors and the shapes of these things; the way they operate consistently in order and in place. The power these things possess is incredible, which makes our assessment of its creator accurate when we say ALMIGHTY.

There are people that care about things such as trees, the ocean, plants, and animals. Why? Do you think a person just loves and cares about trees or the ocean just for their own satisfaction? No way. Whether it's the air we breathe, or the food we eat, that compassion— that love— was placed inside of them from the beginning, by something much bigger than them. Life can be a full-blown mystery; no one has all the answers, but this is what makes our journey interesting and worth living.

It's an experience with ups and downs, hills and valleys, twist and turns, high points and, unfortunately, some low points, but we make it through.

I remember watching an interview with the Oscar Award Winning Actor, Jamie Foxx.

Jamie is one of the most talented actors, singers, and artists of our time. He said when he was a kid, his grandmother took him in. She made sure he stayed busy all the time, especially after school. She made Jamie play sports by having him join the football team, where he eventually became one of the top football players at his high school as a quarterback. After football practice, he would have to hurry home so his grandmother could teach him how to play the piano. According to Jamie, he hated playing the piano, but little did he know, the purpose was much bigger than him.

Later on in life, Jamie had become a great actor, which landed him in one of his first big movie roles playing a what? A QUARTERBACK! He was able to deliver an excellent performance in the hit movie, *Any Given Sunday*. Playing in the quarterback role came as second nature to Jamie; and he was overjoyed about playing this role. This was huge for him. Now, I mentioned earlier how his grandmother made him try out for the football team. At the time, Jamie was only interested because he thought this would be a good way to meet girls. What he didn't know was that he was much bigger than he knew and that his purpose was much greater.

Let us go a bit further. Well, Jamie Foxx completed *Any Given Sunday*, and it was a hit. However, it was nothing like his next movie deal. In 2004, Jamie Foxx set the film industry, and the movie theatres across the nation, on fire with his Oscar Award Winning performance in the movie *Ray*. Jamie shook the world as he embodied the character of the late, great, Ray Charles.

Jamie's Grandmother would pop Jamie's fingers with a ruler at rehearsals when he was a kid for not hitting the right key, or having his hands set the wrong way. I am sure he, or his grandmother, had absolutely no idea that this was all for a purpose much bigger than him. Playing the role of a blind piano player, I'm sure, was challenging, but not as challenging for someone who was predestined to play the role - even before they knew it. WOW! Talk about divine timing at its BEST!!!!

Even our purpose in life is much bigger than us. What I mean by that, and what I have been saying throughout this whole book is, never think it's all about you. This journey is about life, its systems, programs, and functions keep us all moving forward, learning how to coexist here together. We are here to use our own lives as a means to help one another grow, through a multitude of amazing experiences. Your gifts and talents were given to you to make room for you; however, you must share them. YES! Share your gifts and talents with the world creating a better future and legacy.

The Bible tells us, "Be fruitful and multiply." The funny thing is I grew up thinking that meant have a bunch of children; however, when the Bible speaks about children, it uses the word offspring or seed. Additionally, phrases like fruits of our labor are clearly not referring to children. Thus, being fruitful and multiplying simply means to BE PRODUCTIVE in all that you do. Live a life of adding value to someone else, and in return, you will be adding to yours. As my Awesome mentor, Mr. Joel Coppadge Sr. would say, "Whatever you do little bro, GIVE GOD GLORY ALWAYS!!" I would turn to him, smile and say, "AMEN." I think it is very important that we never forget that....

We are all Connected

Whether we are following our passions, building relationships, or freeing ourselves from fear, we have a greater purpose in this world. We may not always understand why we received our abilities, but we must learn to follow the path towards our greater purpose. Mind SET GO gives us a roadmap towards this purpose. It lights our way. It gives us strength and a greater understanding of ourselves. Once we understand and know ourselves, we can show others how to pursue their purpose in this world.

We all have our differences whether it's race, nationality, or creed; however, it's what we have in common that can and will bring us together. One thing for sure, we're all here on this planet trying to create for ourselves a better quality of life. Let us follow peace and love, staying conscious-minded and present, enjoying the best things that life has to offer, claiming and knowing it's our right to live out our purpose and to be fulfilled.

I say, Let us be beautiful together.

"When we know better, we grow better."

MIND SET... now GO!

Made in the USA
Columbia, SC
21 April 2018